Diné Masculinities

Conceptualizations and Reflections

Lloyd L Lee Ph.D.

Cover Art: Image by Diné artist Venaya Yazzie. Pastel on paper. Title: "Holy One-Being"

Copyright © 2013 Lloyd L Lee Ph.D.
All rights reserved.
ISBN: 148234078X
ISBN 13: 9781482340785
Library of Congress Control Number: 2013902627
Createspace Independent Publishing Platform
North Charlestons, South Carolina

Dedicated to Clara B. and Frank M. Lee

'Ahéhee', Shimá dóó shizhe'é

Contents

Acknowledgements

This study has been an interesting and wonderful experience. The time and effort put into this research and the many individuals that have crossed my path to help me along this journey are beyond words. First, this journey began when I was a mere child in Albuquerque, New Mexico, where a lanky and shy boy took notice of what it meant to be Diné (Navajo). Family, friends, and teachers mentored and helped me along my educational journey, and in this process, they did something that is very powerful to any human being. They gave me the encouragement to do well and to be happy in life. Without this encouragement and love, I do not know where my path would have taken me. My mother pushed me to learn and go to school. She and my father went to a five-year vocational training program at Intermountain school in the late 1950s and early 1960s. Both of my parents did not want me to experience that type of education. They wanted me to graduate from high school and go to college. Well, I did accomplish their dreams and more. Without my parents being the foundation of my life, I would not have many accomplishments including the writing of this book.

Second, I would like to thank my fifth grade teacher, Mrs. Hall, and my English teacher in high school, Mrs. Gonzales, as two of the most important elementary and secondary teachers who mentored and pushed me to excel. They are the type of human beings who care and love their students and want them to succeed. Third, I would like to thank Colleen Larimore, Julie Ratico, Michael Hanitchak, Russell Thornton, Colin Calloway, and other individuals at Dartmouth College for providing support through the challenging times. I never imagined a shy and lanky boy from New Mexico attending an Ivy League institution and graduating. Also, I need to thank my friends who were part of the Native Americans at Dartmouth (NAD) student group who made me laugh and helped me endure the difficult experiences of college.

At Stanford University, where I graduated with a master's in education, I need to thank Jim Larimore for his friendship and laughter. I need to also thank the Native American Cultural Center, fellow Native American graduate students, students and faculty with the teacher education program who helped shape my perspective on the education of young people. At the University of New Mexico, I need to thank Amanda Cobb, Gabriel Melendez, Anita Pfeiffer, Bazan Romero, Mary Alice Tsosie, Jennifer Denetdale, Glenabah Martinez, Lee Francis, Gregory Cajete, Beverly Singer, Maria Williams, Mary Bowannie, and numerous others who mentored and supported me during my doctoral program.

At Arizona State University, an internal New College of Interdisciplinary Arts and Sciences grant led me to begin this study. Thank you to Peterson Zah, James Riding In, Myla Vicenti Carpio, Gloria Cuadraz, Jennifer Dorsey, Eduardo Pagan, Karen Leong, Richard Morris, Beverly Honanie, and other individuals who assisted me along this journey. Their friendship and knowledge has influenced me to shape my personal and professional life. I am very appreciative of the support and work of Brendan Hokowhitu, Vincent Diaz, and Ty Tengan; their work on indigenous masculinities is an inspiration to me and without their work I would not have a path to follow.

Thanks to the Indigenous Scholars in Dialogue for Critical Consciousness at the University of New Mexico—Glenabah Martinez, Tiffany Lee, Jennifer Denetdale, Ann Calhoun, Paul Platero, Leola Tsinnijinnie, Beverly Singer—for willingly reading drafts of various chapters. Thank you to the Native American Studies staff and faculty—Delia Halona, Gregory Cajete, Beverly Singer, Tiffany Lee, Mary Bowannie, and Maria Williams—for their support and camaraderie. Thanks to the people who attended the Navajo Studies Conference in 2006 and 2007 at the University of New Mexico and Diné College for their feedback on the various presentations focusing on this issue of Diné masculinities. Last, but not least of all, I want to thank Jeanette Deschenie for editing the words in this book and for listening to and commenting on my thoughts. Without Jeanette's support, I would not have believed in myself enough to write this book. I am truly fortunate to have family, friends, and colleagues who have encouraged, mentored, and supported the work I have done. Ahéhee'.

1
Introduction

When I was a boy I never asked my parents or relatives what it meant to be Diné. Although I am Diné, I do not speak the language fluently, but I have been learning how to speak it for the past twenty years, and I am hopeful I will be able to speak it fluently in the very near future. My parents and relatives speak the language on a daily basis. I attend various ceremonies during the spring, summer, fall, and winter seasons. I listen to various coyote and animal stories told by relatives, medicine people, and others. I live Diné culture, yet I cannot comprehensively define a Diné matrix through the language.[1] I never thought much of a Diné matrix until college. In college, I met other indigenous peoples from around the country and learned about their histories, cultures, and matrices. I learned concepts such as tribal sovereignty, nation building, colonization, decolonization, and identity. My college experience gave me a better understanding of my Diné identity and what all indigenous peoples are fighting to protect.

After college and graduate school, I taught social studies courses at Fort Wingate High School to predominantly Diné students between the ages of fourteen and eighteen. Many of them did not know the history, culture, and language of their own people. Consequently, I made a commitment to teach Diné history and a Diné way of life. I recognized some students wanted to know their history and culture, while others felt they had no use for it. I met parents who held similar viewpoints as their children. I pondered how I, as a Diné man, could ensure the continuance of Diné history and its way of life, language, and thought. After considerable thought and observation of Diné youth, I decided to enroll in a doctorate program to study Diné identity and to use research as a way to ensure Diné continuance.

During my doctoral program, I thought about the type of project I could work on to examine Diné identity. I chose to investigate cultural identity among

Navajo college graduates and college students. The study showed young Diné people are expressing their cultural identity in a diverse and familiar way. Language, philosophy, relationships, and pride and respect define what it means to be Diné for the individuals in my doctoral study. Furthermore, a college education impacts each Diné person in different capacities. For some, college greatly enhances their lives. For others, it reinforces their cultural identity, while others experience minimal effect, but later in life it might have a tremendous influence. Diné identity in the twenty-first century is continuing in an old and fresh way. During the doctoral study, I also began to internally examine my own perspective as a Diné person, more precisely as a Diné man.

I thought about my father's teachings and conduct. Initially, I did not dwell upon cultural knowledge of Diné masculinities, but after further reflection, I realized my father taught me much of what it means to be a Diné man. He taught me what it means to love, and about his desire for his son to be successful and happy.

My father models how to be a Diné man. He never expresses what it means to be Diné and does not tell me many historical stories about Diné male characters, yet I recognize the many traits of a Diné man. A Diné man is one who loves and supports his family. He is a man who overcomes challenges in life. He is a respectful man who does not want more than what is needed. He is a quiet man who provides detailed information when needed. He never physically abuses his wife or his children. He loves his family unconditionally. He is a man who works on a daily basis, even on weekends. He is a strong man. He recognizes he is one component of a complementary partnership. He is not a complete human being without his partner. He is criticized at times by family and friends, but never hurts or shows spite in retaliation. He does everything in life for his family and never asks for anything in return. He is a humble man. This realization guides me in the project.

This book is a study on Diné masculinities focusing on male development and performance, which documents the impact colonization has had on Diné men. The goal of this work is to be transformative and to ensure that future Diné generations will have access to cultural histories, knowledge, and matrices. I acknowledge Jennifer Denetdale's call for transformative work in *Reclaiming Diné History: The Legacies of Navajo Chief Manuelito and Juanita*. In her manuscript, she theorizes ways to revalue Diné philosophy and uphold Diné sovereignty. This book gives testimony to Diné spirits and their efforts to restore a matrix fragmented by colonization. The following questions frame my research:

(1) How are Diné masculinities defined?

(2) How has colonization altered Diné masculinities?

These questions address Diné male identity, development, performance, and transformation. I focus on these areas to initiate dialogue on Diné masculinities. My primary investigation focuses on my discussion with thirty Diné men, whose experiences reflect a combination of Diné thought and an American education. A man's upbringing and family is core to his personal identity. Diné men adopted American perspectives on performance and male roles, however Diné thought is still embedded in each of the thirty men. Colonization and the traumatic consequences have had an impact on Diné men in general, and each man's perspective reflects the degree of impact with regard to various issues.

Although a mixed methods strategy provides a greater comprehensive understanding of Diné masculinities, an interdisciplinary method of narrative research, indigenous storytelling, and gendering yield a distinct perspective on Diné masculinities. Linda Tuhiwai Smith in *Decolonizing Methodologies: Research and Indigenous Peoples* lists twenty-five different indigenous projects to help indigenous peoples control and direct research in their own societies and communities. Smith depicts storytelling as a collective experience in which every indigenous person has a place. The story and the storyteller both serve to connect the past with the future, one generation with the other, the land with the people, and the people with the story.[2] The thirty men in this study share the same attitudes, beliefs, and values in the telling of their collective stories. These men provide thoughts on Diné masculinities. They offer an opportunity to understand the impact of colonization on Diné peoples. According to Smith, the indigenous project of gendering focuses on the relationships between men and women. The project encourages debates to fully discuss destructive effects on gender relations in all spheres of indigenous communities.[3] Diné peoples, and many indigenous peoples, have damaged relationships between men and women based on the consequences of colonization. Building on the foundation of these thirty men openly and honestly discussing their views on life and relationships, Diné communities can openly and honestly communicate about the current problems between men and women. Communication can lead to healing. It is hoped that this research can help promote a dialogue between Diné men and women to help decolonize and rebuild Diné communities.

While the methodology chosen to research Diné masculinities might be a standard approach, the stories and views of the thirty men reflect an understanding of the vitality of Diné peoples and facilitates simple improvements to their lives and uplifts their spirits. These thirty men have valuable insight to offer the Diné and nonindigenous world. They offer their stories and distinct perspectives on being a hastiin (elder man). Diné peoples have adapted to their physical and social environment since creation and the traumatic impact of colonialism and the intrusion on a Diné way of life is a fact that cannot be ignored or forgotten.

I began this Diné masculinities project with many ideas on what to investigate. I realized initially there were many angles to tackle. Early on in the process, the areas of male development and performance, as in other American masculinity studies, stood out. Male development is key to understanding how Diné men define their personal identity. Male performance reflects how Diné men view masculinity and how they relate to other men. Diné history needed to be a part of the study; many changes have occurred in the last two hundred-plus years. The consequences of colonization on Diné peoples must be a part of any examination of gender.

I do briefly discuss the concept of gender in Diné thought, yet a comprehensive investigation in the area of Navajo gender and sexuality is not the focus of this book. Homosexuality is tied to heterosexuality and Euro-American notions of both have influenced and shaped Diné men, such as homophobia. The Diné concept of nádleehé provides a glimpse into Diné thought distinct from the bifurcated notions of masculinity and femininity within Western thought. Diné masculinities are defined on Diné terms and nádleehé is part of Diné concepts of gender and sexuality.

The philosophical principle of Sa'ah Naagháí Bik'éh Hózhǫ́ǫ́n (SNBH) is related to the concepts of masculinity and femininity from a Western notion. However, I feel a comprehensive discussion on this philosophical principle can lead the book on a tangent. I want the focus of the book to be on the Diné male perspectives. Furthermore, in order to have a complete grasp of this thought a person must pursue the dialogue in the Diné language. That is not possible in this book, therefore I do not comprehensively discuss SNBH, but I do have a discussion of the impact of SNBH on Diné masculinities.

I do not include a detailed discussion of relationships between Diné men and women, however I do include brief observations and comments about relationships in the areas of government and marriage. Moreover, I do not include a sociological perspective on the impacts of alcoholism and domestic violence on masculinities, though I briefly discuss both in relation to views on respect toward Diné women. I did decide to include a discussion on the ideals of Diné masculinities based on the stories of the Diyin Dine'é (Holy People) and the twin protectors. Additionally, I discuss the changes to Diné male roles and responsibilities in the last two hundred-plus years.

The thirty Diné men who took part in this study represent many areas of Diné masculinities. I spoke with elders, the young, those who speak the Diné language, those who do not, those who went to college, those who did not, those who were in the military, those who were not, those who are married, and those who are not. I met each Diné man through friends and colleagues. While this study is by no means comprehensive and exhaustive, I feel the thoughts and perspectives of these men represent the numerous views of Diné men. I developed new friendships, which I hope will continue for the rest of my life. These thirty men kindly opened their hearts and thoughts to me. I thank them for their willingness to share with the world. Diné masculinities have changed in the last two hundred-plus years, but these thirty men illustrate how a Diné matrix is intertwined with American attitudes, values, and beliefs.

While each of the thirty men have different thoughts on what it means to be a Diné man, their diversity reflects a key component of Diné identity. Today, many Diné peoples comment on the disagreements and the envy eroding the foundation of Diné society. In contrast, in speaking with these thirty men I find Diné peoples have a strong cohesion. I am hopeful the viewpoints and thoughts of these thirty men illuminate how a Diné matrix exists within an American way of life.

Chapter two lays the groundwork for investigating Diné masculinities with a discussion of various insightful studies on American masculinities, indigenous masculinities, Diné male development, and a discussion of the concept of nádleehé and Diné perspectives on gender and sexuality. Chapter three tells the stories of First Man and First Woman, Changing Woman's twin sons, and the history of Diné peoples. Chapter four discusses the foundational image of Diné masculinities focusing on male responsibilities and the male puberty ceremony. Chapter five focuses on the thirty Diné men who discuss male development, performance, and colonization. Chapter six documents six specific changes to Diné masculinities and has a discussion on contemporary relationships between Diné men and women. The final chapter reflects on the views of the thirty men and discusses the implications for the future. While more needs to be investigated, this research is a starting point.

Diné Masculinities: Conceptualizations and Reflections offers one perspective on Diné masculinities and how Diné men define what it means to be a hastiin. The book also reveals the changing nature of Diné communities. Through these interviews, Diné individuals and groups will be able to see how crucial the status of Diné masculinities is to the health of the Navajo Nation. Throughout the last two hundred-plus years, Diné men never lost sight of fundamental principles for a hastiin. While this book does not cover everything about Diné men, it begins the process of understanding the changes to Diné masculinities and the similarities of historical and contemporary meanings. The book is offered in the hopes that future Diné scholars will further investigate other key issues impacting Diné men. This study begins with one man, one hastiin with the expectations other hastiins will follow.

2
Nitsáhákees:
Thinking of Diné Masculinities

Each Diné man establishes their masculinity in distinctive and diverse ways. Walter Johnson, age thirty-seven, describes the Diné male role as demonstrated, "By being in control and having a logical reason behind it. By being a disciplinarian, doing male type chores, i.e., cutting wood. Passing cultural knowledge and practicing ceremonies."[1] Peter Walker, age twenty-seven, offers a different perspective. "I try to improve on my life every day. I wake up and strive to get something accomplished every day whether it is for me, my family, or outside community. I also try to research, study, and learn about Diné history and worldviews. I try to follow what customs and spirituality I was taught. I'm not perfect and have not always lived my life like this, but maturing is a part of becoming a man."[2] These men take dissimilar approaches in answering the question of what it means to be a Diné man. Each individual Diné has a perspective, which is representative of a diverse Navajo Nation. Some Diné men are part of the ongoing effort to rebuild the Navajo Nation, maintaining or revitalizing the language, continuing ceremonial participation, or teaching communal knowledge. Others are not.

Since the mid-nineteenth century, Diné men and peoples have lived in an American world. While maturity and growth is part of Diné history, it still has been a difficult and challenging process for the people. The creation narratives help the people work through many challenges and adversities. These stories tell of the challenges and dilemmas the peoples endured in various prior ways of life. The stories of survival and trauma also help the peoples to understand the consequences of colonialism. Anthropologist John R. Farella describes the dilemma for Diné peoples in coping with the consequences of colonialism:

Navajos know very well about all levels of adaptation—eco-
logical, social, and personal. In addition, they see it as basically the same process, and regard themselves as part of, not
separate from it. They also happen to be very good at adaptation. But, most important, they know it is a risky business. On
the level of a society, an old way can disappear; at the level
of the individual, personal growth can lead to one's literal or
symbolic death. Navajos certainly feel sadness for and mourn
such happenings, but they are not very surprised by them.[3]

Diné men have been forced to adopt various aspects of Euro-American
customs, values, attitudes, and beliefs such as practicing Christianity, speaking and writing English, and watching television. For millennia, Diné peoples
have created and infused other peoples' technologies, customs, and beliefs and
molded these concepts into a distinct Diné way of life. This infusion does not
mean the people have never created original knowledge, instead they have
maintained a vibrant way of life. This also means Diné peoples are not cultural
borrowers as often claimed by some anthropologists, but peoples who use their
creativity and adaptability. The relationship of the people to the earth is one of
respect and reciprocity. The people have been able to maintain their way of life
for the most part, even as Euro-American colonialism altered many aspects of
Diné thought and way of life.

Prior to colonization, Diné communities did not distinguish between male
and female through a gender order or power relations between groups of people. Male and female essences are thought to be part of all living entities in the
universe. For instance, the earth is referred to as Nahasdzáán Shimá (Mother
Earth) and the universe as Yádiłhił Shitaa' (Father Sky). In Diné thought, the
philosophical principle of SNBH represents the pursuit of happiness and the
striving for stability. SNBH is crucial energy for sustaining life in the universe.
Sa'ah Naagháí is male and Bik'eh Hózhǫ is female. Sa'ah Naagháí and Bik'eh
Hózhǫ came from First Man's medicine bundle. They became the parents of
Changing Woman, who represents the power of reproduction, and beauty in
this world. Changing Woman created the four original clans of the Diné peoples. The dynamic union of Sa'ah Naagháí and Bik'eh Hózhǫ creates Hózhǫ
(beauty, balance, and harmony). Diné men and women strive for Hózhǫ in life.

Since Changing Woman created the people and is made from SNBH, all Diné men and women have both male and female energies in their system.

While specific Diné terms in the language designate male and female, they are understood in terms of individuality within a collective. Diné men and women have duties and responsibilities to fulfill for their community's sustainability. While men and women live their own individual lives, their identities are not exclusive of the community. Their matrix ensures a respectful relationship with all living entities on earth and in the universe. The differences between men and women are also acknowledged. For instance, these differences are commonly heard and seen through the language. The language does not encode a specific gender. Married men are called hastiin, and married women are ʼasdzáán. A young boy is called ʼashkii, and a young girl is ʼatʼééd. Boys are called ʼashiiké and girls ʼatʼééké. Gender difference is not based on a gender order or on power relations between groups, but rather by name, relationship, and life cycle, which connects other men, women, relatives, and families. So while gender diversity existed in Diné communities before colonialism it was not until the reservation era where in fact major doubts toward gender diversity blossomed among Diné peoples. This change creates a significant shift in how Diné men view their masculinity and their relationship to Diné women. How do Diné men differ from American men with regard to development, performance, and history?

Numerous masculinity studies in the United States have examined primarily Euro-American, heterosexual, middle-class men. Some studies examined specific ethnic and racial group masculinities such as African Americans and Latinos. However, no masculinity study has ever investigated a specific Native Nation in the United States to find out how indigenous men define and confirm their masculinity and how colonization has impacted their masculinities. Several scholars within indigenous communities, such as Vincent Diaz, Brendon Hokowhitu, and Ty Tengan have researched their respective indigenous nations in Guam, New Zealand, and Hawaii. Their studies have contributed greatly to the studies of indigenous masculinities. One article in particular discusses a Diné male development model familiar to Diné peoples.

In "Becoming a Medicine Man: A Means to Successful Midlife Transition among Traditional Navajo Men," Martin D. Topper and G. Mark Schoepfle examine how Diné men develop into hataałiis (healers). They describe a Diné male development paradigm, though they do not discuss the impact of colonization on male development. Although Topper and Schoepfle's interpretation can help readers understand a particular Diné male development model, theorizing on the construction of Diné male identity must include the history of the people and the way the people live, which includes how colonialism has altered Diné communities. Nonetheless, a description and analysis of the paradigm is warranted.

Stage one ('awéé') takes place from birth to age two. The baby is passive and very dependent on the mother and father. Stage two ('ashkii yázhi) takes place from age two to puberty. The young boy will go through four steps of mental development in this stage. The first step, háni' hazlíí, is where the young boy becomes aware of immediate surroundings and is no longer a baby but a child. For many people, this step is where people first remember. In the second step, ádaa' ákozhniidzíí, he becomes self-aware. The young boy, who is usually between four and six years old, becomes more aware of the environment through the stories told in the hogan, the four elements of life, and Mother Earth. The child begins to learn about K'é and K'éí, the Navajo relationship and clanship systems. He learns the proper and respectful way to address family and relatives. He is taught how to have respect for nature and all living entities. The second step is where the child begins to understand specific roles and responsibilities modeled by their parents and elders. Parents during this time begin to teach their child how to wake up before sunrise, pray, meditate, exercise, and to show respect for elders.

In the third step, nitsídzíkees dzizlíí', the young boy begins to think and behave independently. During this step, which occurs between the ages of six and nine, he gets up before sunrise, runs toward the east, prays, and offers yellow cornmeal. The boy also learns to offer white cornmeal at sunset. At this stage, the boy learns to perform household tasks according to the division of labor. Additionally, around this age the child is given a lamb as a gift. The care of the lamb is to teach the child responsibilities.

In the fourth step, hanitsékees niliínii hazlíí', which occurs between the ages of ten and fifteen, the child's thoughts "begin existing." The young boy learns to think in Diné on a constant basis, in other words, cultural knowledge frames his perception of the world. The child's thoughts must be on the environment, the hogan, the cardinal directions, and the land. Around this age, the child is expected to remember and synthesize knowledge gained from the creation narratives. He must learn to plan ahead and apply all knowledge to daily activities such as prayer in the morning and evening. The stories told to the child focus on land, entities, relationships, and responsibility. During this step, the elders will also tell the young boy whether or not he will become a hataałii. In addition, he will be initiated into manhood through the kinaaldá, a puberty ceremony. In the puberty ceremony, he learns how to live as an 'ashkii and later a hastiin. He learns how to sing the proper songs during a sweat, and he learns the expectation of being independent and accepting complete responsibility for his actions.

The third stage of male development is the 'ashkii stage. Three levels make up this stage. The first level, ádá nitsídzíkees dzilíí, occurs between the ages of fifteen and eighteen. Parents remind their son he is no longer a dependent and must take full responsibility for appropriate household and family chores. By this time, his physical qualities are well developed, and he has completed training in enduring hardship and adversity. He is also expected to know the principles of K'é and K'éí completely.

The second level, t'áá altsoní baanitsídzíkees dzilíí', is where the boy begins to think about all things. During this level between seventeen and twenty-two years of age, he develops mastery of all necessary life skills and adult responsibilities. Furthermore, he is deemed ready for marriage and to have a separate and independent household. The young boy is on his way to becoming a hataałii.

The third level, ádá náá nitsídzíkees dzilíí, is where the boy begins to think ahead for himself. He gets married, often through an arrangement, and focuses his energy on protecting and sustaining his new family.

Stage four is the hastiin stage. Thirty to thirty-five years of age is the timeframe where this stage takes place. The final mental development step, t'aa altsoníbá náás nitsídzíkees dzilíí, is where he begins to think ahead for all things. He is ready to be a teacher and leader of others, expressing his views and teaching his children and the children of others the lessons his parents and relatives taught him.

The fifth and final stage in a hataałii's life is hastiin sáni (aged elder male). Usually, men who are over the age of seventy are recognized as hastiin sáni. He is in decline physically and mentally. He depends on his children and grandchildren and is viewed with esteem due to the knowledge and experience he has accumulated.

This Diné development paradigm is still known and lived, yet many Diné men do not want to become a hataałii or have the patience and motivation to do so. Some Diné men do not have the knowledge of this growth model because of the consequences of colonization. Questions asked to the thirty men on male development are based on this paradigm.

Diné perspectives of gender, sexuality, and the concept of nádleehé are also part of male development. In Diné thought, gender is viewed beyond the bifurcated role of male and female, in fact Diné way of life has multiple genders. In addition to male and female, Diné way of life also includes the category of nádleehé. Nádleehé mixes various aspects of the behaviors, activities, and occupations of both females and males.[4] Western thought might use the term hermaphrodite to describe nádleehé. From a Diné perspective, nádleehé refers to characteristics and not biological entities. Diné men who demonstrate characteristics of the opposite gender meet the role of a nádleehé.

The Diné concept of sexuality is in several stories of the creation narratives. For instance, the separation of the sexes story has sexuality as a transparent and interwoven theme. Sexuality is one of the factors behind the separation of men and women and the development of the monsters, who later terrorize Diné peoples. Sexuality is not hidden from view. Diné perceptions of sexuality are tied to living, balance, and reproduction. They are not discussed openly, and sexual relations are always a private matter, but sexuality is tied to the stories and Diné thought.

Diné gender and sexuality are distinct from Western thought. Very little has been written on these two areas. One of the few is Wesley Thomas's "Navajo Cultural Constructions of Gender and Sexuality" in *Two-Spirit People: Native American Gender Thought, Sexuality, and Spirituality*. Thomas's article discusses how Diné culture has had multiple genders and how Diné peoples' perspectives on gender and sexuality have been affected by Euro-American thought and way of life. More research in the area of gender and sexuality is warranted, and as more and more young Diné students attend college and graduate school the opportunity for more written discussion in these two areas will come to fruition.

Tim Edwards, in *Cultures of Masculinity*, highlights the eras in men's studies. Initial male studies focus on the sex role paradigm. As Edwards says, "The key emphasis of these studies was, first, to demonstrate the socially constructed nature of masculinity and its reliance on socialization, sex role learning and social control; and second, to attempt to document how these processes were limiting and perhaps even harmful to men in terms of their own psychological and even physical health."[5] The second wave shifted to criticism of the initial studies and discussing the "contemporary crisis of masculinity." Studies in this second wave propose a pro-feminist approach to studying masculinities. Men's studies also examine the concept of power in relation to women and society and aligning perspectives with feminism. The more recent research has been influence by postcolonialism and post-structural theory, and studies discuss race/ethnicity, performance, and sexuality.

Handbook of Studies on Men and Masculinities, edited by Michael Kimmel, Jeff Hearn, and R.W. Connell, is a comprehensive attempt to cover many areas of men's studies, ranging from theory to politics. Many of the chapters examine the area of male representation and question the concept of change in the gender structure. While masculinity research continues to extend men's studies from the beginning, earlier works define how men's studies have been shaped.

Two scholars who have written extensively on American masculinities are Michael Kimmel and Michael Messner. Kimmel and Messner's scholarship has influenced a significant amount of discussion on American masculinities. Kimmel's research focuses extensively on advocating a pro-feminist approach to men's studies, particularly outlining how men should support women in the fight against gender discrimination and domestic violence. He details how masculinity is an ever-changing, fluid assemblage of meanings and behaviors that vary dramatically.[6] He prefers to use the term masculinities to recognize the different masculinity constructions. I use the plural term masculinities for this research as well. Diné communities are as diverse as America. Diné masculinities are distinct, and each man lives his own life according to the values and beliefs he learns.

Michael Messner's work examines how sport contributes to and impacts masculine identity. He also uses the term masculinities and discusses the construction of masculinities through organized sports. Sports encourages the development of "conditional self-worth" since acceptance from others depends on being a winner.[7] According to Messner, men from lower-status backgrounds tend to view sports in the context of community and their families, and sports becomes the place to construct an identity.

R. W. Connell, a professor at the University of Sydney, is the first to use the term masculinities to describe the different perspectives and understandings of masculinity in *Masculinities*. Kimmel extends the meaning of masculinities to state that pluralizing the term masculinity does not mean all masculinities are equal. He writes, "Typically, each nation constructs a model of masculinity against which each man measures himself."[8] According to Kimmel, masculinity is constructed through the articulation of differences against "others"—racial, ethnic, class, and gender. These differences help construct a hegemonic masculinity. He cites sociologist Erving Goffman, who describes the hegemonic masculine image in 1963:

> In an important sense there is only one complete unblushing male in America: a young, married, white, urban, northern, heterosexual, Protestant, father, of college education, fully employed, of good complexion, weight, and height, and a recent record in sports. Any male who fails to qualify in any one of these ways is likely to view himself—during moments at least—as unworthy, incomplete, and inferior.[9]

Do Diné men construct their masculinity based on differences (Kimmel), or are differences part of the core values in Diné masculinities? Diné men's differences do appear to be a part of Diné identity.

Kimmel utilizes multiple definitions of masculinities, and those masculinities are constructed in relation to femininities and are thus expressed within a gendered order. This gender order is reflected in institutions and the dynamic of power relations between groups. He explains, "the gender order expresses men's power over women (male domination) and the power of some men over other men (by race, sexuality, ethnicity, age, able-bodied-ness)."[10] The gender order helps create an inequitable society where men express their power over women, and heterosexual Euro-American thought dominate the ideology of American masculinity. Diné masculinities are influenced by American ideology. This influence is reflected in the thirty Diné men.

Kimmel, in *Manhood in America*, summarizes the history of heterosexual, middle class Euro-American men in the United States. He begins with the birth of the self-made man in the late eighteenth and early nineteenth centuries. According to Kimmel, the self-made man is a "model of manhood of which identity derived entirely from a man's activities in the public sphere, measured by accumulated wealth and status, by geographic and social mobility."[11] This self-made man is the ideal displacing "the genteel patriarch" and "the heroic artisan." He describes the evolution of the self-made man in the nineteenth century from industrialization to the challenges and confirmation of his masculinity in the areas of sport and leisure. He continues with this analysis to reveal the increasing anxieties men feel in the early and middle parts of the twentieth century. According to Kimmel, American men are preoccupied with demonstrable masculinity. This leads to what he terms the "contemporary crisis of masculinity" where men are searching for the meaning of manliness, and a particular concern is how one proves or demonstrates being "truly manly." He describes how American men employ three strategies to overcome this crisis. First, men seek to control their own bodies and lives. Second, men define themselves by excluding others from the belief of true manhood (the self-made man is a middle class Euro-American man, who casts his ideal image against undesirable African Americans, Native Americans, immigrants, and "sissies"). Third, men escape to where they can be "real" men if all else fails. According to Kimmel, American men have been trying to define what it truly means to be a man for the past two hundred years. Colonization has forced Diné men to follow a similar path. The interviews will show male performance has been influence by American notions of the self-made man and the "contemporary crisis of masculinity."

While Kimmel contextualizes the "contemporary crisis of masculinity," Connell, in *Masculinities*, stresses the need for gender justice. She argues men are still dominant and in control over women, even individual men or groups of men who are confused about their masculinity or have insecurities. Connell frames masculinity through the consolidation of historically situated social practices. These social practices define for men the power they have and how it is displayed. She examines four contrasting groups of Australian men and how the shifting social relations shaped men's everyday activities and experiences. She indicates the body is an inescapable component in the construction of masculine identity. Connell equates the structure of gender and particularly masculinity to power, production, and cathexis (emotional attachment).

While Kimmel, Messner, and Connell theorize on the structure of masculinity based on gender order, sports, power, production, and cathexis, Warren Steinberg, in *Masculinity: Identity Conflict and Transformation*, takes a

Jungian approach in discussing masculine development. Steinberg believes men and women should strive for C. G. Jung's individuation—a drive to integrate the unconscious, unite the opposites, and achieve wholeness.[12] Men need to balance the traditional American masculine qualities with the recognition and acceptance of the anima, or man's inner feminine. According to Steinberg, family and culture is where boys learn to be men, yet American society creates men who do not feel they are "truly men." Boys learn to be men from their fathers. Steinberg explains, "…the son knowingly strives to imitate the characteristics of his father in order to develop his masculine persona."[13] This learned behavior along with understanding man's inner feminine establishes a strong and free masculinity. The traditional masculine qualities of competence, strength, power and instrumental achievement lead to furthering man's ideal of freedom. The ability of the individual man to achieve a better understanding of his identity is the ultimate goal. The ability of the Diné person to achieve a better understanding of his/her identity is based on a matrix whose foundation is balance, wellness, cooperation, and individuality within a communal setting. The thirty men represent this matrix. The Jungian approach has the right idea although the wrong approach. Diné thought has always stipulated a balanced (male and female) approach in life with the individual tied to community. The ultimate goal is maturing one's identity, but tied to community and not separate or on its own.

While Kimmel, Steinberg, Connell, and Messner theorize on male development, other studies have analyzed the display or performance of American masculinities. Varda Burstyn's *The Rites of Men: Manhood, Politics, and the Culture of Sport* describes how sports cultivates hyper masculinities that contribute to misogynistic male behavior. The central thesis states that as a result of political and economic shifts in the industrial parts of Europe and North America, Euro-American families underwent major changes to their way of life. Men found work outside the home and women managed families. Because of this shift, men began to develop certain anxieties, which resulted in the formation of sports as a way to properly socialize boys into normative masculinity. She describes the popularity of sports as a "masculinist secular religion." This "religion" perpetuates a super-aggressive ideal image of masculinity. Sports participation has allowed men to show they are indeed "real men." It is one of the most powerful anchors of masculine identity. Euro-American men believe sports is the framework of who they are and the proof they need in order to confirm their masculinity. Diné communities, increasingly influenced by Euro-American thought, have adopted both rodeo and basketball as part of the way of life.

Wanda Ellen Wakefield extends this idea in *Playing to Win: Sports and the American Military, 1898-1945*. She describes how the American military, from 1898 to World War II, developed a comprehensive, formal sports program. This sports program became a way for the US military to create a fighting force to dominate the battlefield. Sports became a mechanism for the military to create overall discipline and reinforce the organizational hierarchy. Men learned how to fight in war by participating in sports. Wakefield argues cultural constructions of aggressive masculinity and superiority became the driving forces behind sports competitions. War and sports were synonymous and both became a way to display American masculinities. Wakefield elaborates on the American military rationale and purpose for the individual man. The individual man in the military learns to fight in war and compete in sports. Many Diné men and women serve in the US military, and there is a long history of Diné people defending and fighting for the United States.

While sports and military participation are two ways American masculinities perform, fatherhood is another way to express one's masculinity. In *Fatherhood Politics in the United States: Masculinity, Sexuality, Race, and Marriage*, Anne Gavanas details the fatherhood responsibility movement in the United States in the 1980s and 1990s. The central concern of the movement is to confront and overcome the difficulty men face as they struggle to determine their role as fathers in domestic life. She describes United States fatherhood politics including pro-marriage and fragile-family sections, religion and sports metaphors, and sexual politics in the movements. Her premise is men reshape and reconfirm their masculinity by competing and bonding with other men. Men bond with other men via sports, religion, courtship, and work. The pro-marriage section concentrates on moral obligations and cultural values, promoting marriage as central to the "culture of fatherhood."[14] Most members in this section are white Euro-American men. The members emphasize gender and sexual differences. Marriage proponents want to reinforce more or less essentialist notions of gender and parental difference and cement those differences within the institution of marriage.[15] This section also relies on the Bible to support many of its tenets. Pro-marriage advocates argue men play specific roles as fathers and are responsible for parenting the children. Only fathers have the authority to curb their sons' destructive and violent behavior, and only parental responsibility tied to marital commitment can truly domesticate men into responsible fathers.[16]

The fragile-families section takes a different approach to the subject of fatherless families. This section sees the problem with competition from other men. It argues minority men do not have the same access to sufficient resources to help them marry. Rather than promoting marriage, this section encourages "team parenting" as the most crucial step in raising a child. Parental involvement in a child is the most important factor, rather than merely being married. Whereas marriage is a key issue for the pro-marriage section, work is key in the fragile-families section.[17] Fatherhood strengthens what it means to be a man. In Diné communities, fatherhood is discussed at the boy's puberty ceremony. He learns the importance of taking care of a child and his responsibility. This responsibility equates to love, which is often not equated to American masculinities, but in Diné communities, love is connected to happiness, prosperity, and balance.

In *The Will to Change: Men, Masculinity, and Love*, the author bell hooks argues men are longing for love, and patriarchal society denies a man's feelings. hooks analyzes the stages of a man's life through babyhood, boyhood, teenage years, and adulthood. She believes patriarchy plays a significant role in sociosexual ills, and men seek alienating sex as a substitute for the love unavailable to them. She explains, "Sex, then becomes for most men a way of self-solacing. It is not about connecting to someone else but rather releasing their own pain."[18] Men need to search for love not through sex, but rather through love itself. Love can release a man's pain. The path to love is when a man chooses to become emotionally aware. Women must help men realize this love. hooks writes:

> The work of male relational recovery, of reconnection, of forming intimacy and making community can never be done alone. In a world where boys and men are daily losing their way we must create guides, signposts, and new paths. A culture of healing that empowers males to change is in the making. Healing does not take place in isolation. Men who love and men who long to love know this. We need to stand by them, with open hearts and open arms. We need to stand ready

to hold them, offering a love that can shelter their wounded spirits as they seek to find their way home, as they exercise the will to change.[19]

The hegemonic masculine identity established by heterosexual, upper class, Euro-American men has set the standards for how American men are to live, think, and act, whereas love is often not associated with American masculinities. Instead, American masculinities are frequently equated within Euro-American colonialism. Euro-American men created America, and indigenous men experienced the consequences of colonialism. Historical accounts from travelers, diplomats, military officers, and others mentioned indigenous masculinities but indigenous creation narratives provide the groundwork for pertinent social mechanisms and cultural frameworks for indigenous men.

Brendon Hokowhitu, a professor at the University of Otago in New Zealand, has studied Maori masculinities. In "Tackling Maori Masculinity: A Colonial Genealogy of Savagery and Sport," Hokowhitu describes the stereotype of Maori (or Tane) men as natural sportsmen:

> The myth of the natural athleticism of Maori men has been actuated through tane achieving in sport more than in any other areas of society—so much so that sport has come to be viewed as a "traditional" characteristic of Maori masculinity. Ironically, many aspects of Maori masculinity now regarded as traditional were merely selected qualities of British colonial masculinity. In hopes of saving their people from near extinction, many tane were forced to assume those masculine qualities that would abet their integration into the dominant Pakeha culture. The consumption of Pakeha masculinity by tane served to assimilate them into the violent, physical, stoical, rugged, and sports-oriented mainstream masculine world that has pervaded New Zealand society for most of its colonial history.[20]

According to Hokowhitu, some Maori men accept non-Maori views of what makes a tane. This acceptance has lead to myths about Maori masculinities. Some Maori men do not accept how physicality determines the meaning of a tane. The educational movements of Kohanga reo (preschool, total-immersion language nests) and Kura Kauapapa (primary and high schools based on tikanga Maori and total language immersion) are helping to change the mindset of some Maori men. The men are learning the significance of whanaungatanga (family), hinengaro (intellect), wairua (spirituality), aroha (love and compassion), and manaakitanga (support and concern for others). The history of the Maori peoples illustrates the forced incorporation of colonialist attitudes, beliefs, and values; even then Maori communities are taking the initiative to decolonize their peoples.

All indigenous nations in the Western hemisphere have traumatically changed in the past five hundred years. Kim Anderson's *A Recognition of Being: Reconstructing Native Womanhood* and Ty P. Kawika Tengan's dissertation "Hale Mua: (En)Gendering Hawaiian Men" describe how Euro-American colonization changed indigenous communities in Canada and Hawaii, and in turn altered indigenous men.

Anderson encourages First Nations women in Canada to engage in a process of self-definition encompassing the concepts of resist, reclaim, construct, and act. The idea is for indigenous women to follow a strategy to heal the pain and burden of colonization. She investigates how indigenous women were positioned in Aboriginal communities and traces European colonization on First Nations. For instance, she discusses the power indigenous women had in traditional politics until the Canadian Indian Act dispossessed women of communal authority. The act also dismantled women's authority within the family due to the imposition of the patriarchal institution of marriage and the elimination of property rights. She explains:

> For over a century, Native women were shut out of their communities and families. Women who kept their status were shut out of political and economic decision-making because they were restricted from owning property. Even on the death of their husbands they had no inheritance rights: "On the death of an Indian, his 'goods and chattels' and land rights were to be passed to his children. The wife was excluded, her maintenance being the responsibility of the children."[21]

Anderson also discusses the dismantling of First Nations women's spiritual power and the construction of a negative female image. Native women experienced negative changes in family, spirituality, and sexuality. She narrates how Christian ideology condemned Native women's sexuality:

> It became shame-based and subject to scrutiny and punishment by the church. Barbara-Helen Hill recounts the puritanical teachings around sex that replaced our traditional teachings. Native women, she writes, were told that sex is "a man's thing; men enjoy it; it's a woman's duty; it's dirty; save yourself for your husband." Traditional teachings, which encouraged a healthy sexuality, were erased.[22]

Anderson extensively narrates how colonization changed First Nations, particularly the positive images of Native women. She advocates a strategy of resist, reclaim, construct, and act to reverse the negative consequences.

Tengan takes a similar approach in highlighting how Kanaka Maoli (Hawaiian) men transform, redefine, and enact their subjectivities as indigenous men. Tengan's study entails how colonization altered Kanaka Maoli communities and how a small number of men formed the Hale Mua, or Men's House, on the island of Maui to build a strong, culturally grounded group, which upholds the responsibilities of their families and nation. He summarizes how Kanaka Maoli men participated in the military and in sports. At the same time, they are returning to traditional institutions to help maintain and strengthen Kanaka Maoli masculinities. They are practicing male traditions borrowed or influenced by Maori. Kanaka Maoli men viewed this as a shared Polynesian culture between families. Tengan writes, "The important part of this claim is that masculinity is identified with authentic traditions of precolonial Polynesian society that were able to resist the perceived feminization and emasculation that accompanied colonization in Hawaii."[23] This resistance does not equate to a balanced gender relationship. Kanaka Maoli men are still struggling to create a decolonized mind-set.

Tengan illustrates how the Hale Mua is an attempt to build a strong culturally based nation, which models the idea of 'pono.' 'Pono' is a Kanaka Maoli principle of balance, well-being, and righteous gender relations. This attempt to regain and restructure aspects of Kanaka Maoli teachings to create a masculine identity as found prior to European colonization is challenging and difficult. Both Anderson and Tengan depict changes to indigenous communities and the attempts by indigenous peoples to reclaim their cultural matrices.

Diné communities have similar experiences. These studies provide background information on development, performance, and the impact of colonization on indigenous men. The following chapters will show how Diné men construct and display their masculinity and how colonization altered Diné communities, specifically examining the changes to Diné masculinities in the last two hundred-plus years.

3
History of Diné Masculinities

In time, she had twins. Both were boys. As the boys grew up,
their mother adored them and gave them much love. When
they still were small, they had their first bows and arrows.
They would go hunting for small game and bring back rabbits and squirrels. The boys exercised daily, wrestling and
running. They would race to the east to the top of a mountain
in the morning. There they would breathe in the sunlight as
it came out from behind the mountains to the east. When it
snowed, they would roll in the snow, stripped of their clothing. Soon they were very strong.[1]

The epigraph is a description from the Diné creation narratives, specifically,
the story of Changing Woman and her twin sons born in the fourth or fifth
world depending on which version you read or heard. Changing Woman's twin
sons represent the ideal images of Diné men.

Diné men learn the meaning of a hastiin from a Diné way of life and the
creation narratives. The stories of First Man and the twin sons exemplify for
Diné men how to live and to understand their responsibilities to their families
and communities. The image of the ideal Diné man derives from these stories,
but actual life experiences have proven not all Diné men achieve this image.
This chapter will focus on the stories of First Man and Changing Woman's
twin sons and contextualize Diné masculinities from the sixteenth to the twenty-first centuries. The version told in this chapter is from the book *Navajo*

History Volume I compiled by the Navajo Curriculum Center, edited by Ethelou Yazzie, and published by Rough Rock Press in 1971.

Áltsé Hastiin aadóó Áltsé 'Asdzą́ą́

The story of Áltsé hastiin (First Man) and Áltsé 'asdzą́ą́ (First Woman) in this section is one perspective. Different perspectives on the creation narratives exist, and I do not wish to state one version is more correct than another. The different narrative versions reflect the diversity of Diné peoples. This version is general and has been written by several non-Navajo studies scholars. Diné men and women learn life begins with the First World's creation and Áltsé hastiin and Áltsé 'asdzą́ą́.

In the eastern area of the First World, white and black clouds mixed and formed Áltsé hastiin and white corn. In the western area of the world, yellow and blue clouds mixed and formed Áltsé 'asdzą́ą́ and yellow corn. Along with First Man and First Woman, two other entities (angry coyote and coyote formed in water) were created in the First World. The First World was dark, and they decided to move into the Second World. They continued their journeys into the Third and Fourth Worlds. Each journey into the different worlds brought new encounters with different entities. The life lessons learned in each world formed the ethics and standards Diné peoples are supposed to follow now.

While First Man is not an actual human being—in fact, he is a Holy Being—the principles he lived by are what Diné men strive towards. The life principles taught from the stories of First Man include sustenance, courage, responsibility, respect, hospitality, knowledge, and wellness. First Man and First Woman taught these principles to 'Asdzą́ą́ Nádleehé (Changing Woman).

Hozhǫ́ is the path for living. Many explanations for Hozhǫ́ focus on the concept of "walking in beauty." The individual strives to live a balance life, to acknowledge and respect positive and negative energies. The stories of First Man and First Woman show Diné men and women life will be challenging. For instance, when male and female entities separated in the Third World, First Man and First Woman realized they could not live apart because they needed each other to sustain life. This story teaches Diné men and women in this world the appropriate and respectful way to live together. Changing Woman's twin sons also emulate the way Diné men must strive to live.

Naayéé' Neezghání, Tó Bájísh Chíní, aadóó Jóhonaa'éí

Naayéé' Neezghání (Monster Slayer), the older brother, was braver and more daring, while Tó Bájísh Chíní (Child Born of Water), the younger brother, was not as strong. 'Asdzą́ą́ Nádleehé raised both sons without their father. First Man, First Woman, and the Holy People help raised the boys. First Man made them bows and arrows and took them on hunting trips. Haashch'ééshzhin (Fire God) took on the role of their uncle; he was a counselor, teacher, and disciplinarian. The brothers learned to respect their elders, to be self-sufficient within limitations, to not ridicule others, and to avoid poverty. The extended family taught Naayéé' Neezghání and Tó Bájísh Chíní vital life principles.

After a period of time, the twins asked their mother about their father. At first, Changing Woman would not tell them anything. She only said their father was dangerous and could kill them. This only made them more curious.

One day, on a hunting trip, the twins came upon a tiny hole in the ground with smoke drifting out. The boys heard a voice calling them to come in. The hole widen for the boys to crawl in. They climbed down a ladder to the bottom where they reached Na'ashjé'ii 'Asdzą́ą́'s (Spider Woman's) home. Na'ashjé'ii 'Asdzą́ą́'s home was beautiful with webs and feathers from bird types of every description and color. She asked the twins what they were doing, and one of them responded they were on a hunting trip. One of the boys also explained they wanted to find their father so they could ask him for his help to kill the monsters roaming the Earth. Spider Woman responded she knew who their father was, and she could help them find him—their father was Jóhonaa'éí (Sun).

She fed the boys and showed them her great wealth of feathers. She fed the older brother corn meal with a small piece of turquoise in it, and the younger brother the same meal with a small piece of white shell. She also gave each a hiinááh bits'os (magic eagle feather) for protection. The turquoise and white shell were supposed to give the twins courage and make their hearts strong.

She told the twins what they would face during their journey to find their father. The trip would be dangerous and difficult, and she instructed them on what to do as they encountered each challenge. They learned the proper chants and prayers to keep them from harm.

The first challenge was Lok'aa' Adigishii (Reeds that Cut). In order for them to pass this challenge without getting killed, the boys needed to call the reed by the proper name and say the right prayer. The second challenge was Séit'áád (Moving Sand). The moving sand could cover a person if they stepped into it. The boys could cross it only with the proper prayer, chant, and by calling the moving sand by its correct name. The third challenge was Tsé'Ahééninídił (Canyon that closed in on a Traveler). The only way to escape death from the canyon was to use the magic eagle feathers. No prayer or proper chant could help them. The fourth challenge was Tsé Yot'ááhí'aii (Four Pillars of Rocks). These represented old age. She told the boys to pass on the sunny side of the rocks and not the shady side, which would cause them to die of old age. The fifth challenge was Nahodits'ǫ' (Wash that Swallowed). The twins needed to pray and call the wash by its proper name to avoid getting killed—to cross the wash they rode Wóóshiyishí (Measuring Worm). Once the wash reached the ocean, the boys encountered Tółkáá' Dijádii (Water Skeeter). They would need to explain to Water Skeeter why they needed a ride, and also recite a few prayers before they began their journey across the ocean.

Upon reaching the Sun's home, the boys encountered four doormen who guarded the house; Tł'iish tsoh dooniniti'ii (Gigantic Snake), Shashtsoh (Huge Black Bear), Ii'ni'Bika'ii (Big Thunder), and Níyoltsoh (Big Wind). Spider Woman taught the boys the proper chants and prayers to get past these guardians. Once they passed these guardians, they entered their father's home.

The boys overcame each obstacle. They reached their father's house and met his wife. The wife was startled to see the two boys. She questioned them, and the twins responded they wanted to see their father. The wife did not believe them. She became angry and tried to persuade the boys to leave, but they refused. The wife was afraid for their safety, but the boys did not fear for their lives. The Sun returned home and inquired about the two boys entering his home. At first, the Sun's wife did not acknowledge his question, but eventually she chastised him about two boys coming to visit their father. The Sun searched for the two boys and found them. The boys explained their visit, but the Sun refused to believe them. He wanted to test them.

The first test was to smoke tobacco. The Sun prepared a strong smoke designed to kill a human. The boys smoked the tobacco four times and felt fine. The prayers, chants, and magic eagle feather protected the twins from the dangerous smoke.

The second test was to take a sweat bath. The Sun's daughter helped the twins. She dug a pit in the back of the sweat lodge and covered it with sheets of white shell, darkness, evening twilight, sky blue, and dawn. She designed the pit to protect them from the enormous heat her father generated. The boys passed the test, and the Sun thought they were indeed his sons. However, the father subjected the twins to two additional tests: eating poisonous corn meal, and big, sharp, multicolored béésh doolghasii (flint knives). Each time the twins passed the test.

After the four tests, the Sun acknowledged the twins were his sons, and his daughter bathed them. The daughter bathed the twins four times and each time in a different basket: white bead, turquoise, white shell, and black obsidian. The Sun, then molded and shaped the twins, and dressed them in beautiful clothes. The father showed the twins gifts they could take back with them on their journey home. While the twins acknowledged the gifts, they wanted the power to kill the monsters terrorizing the people. Several monsters such as Yé'iitsoh (Big Monster), Déélgééd (Horned Monster), Tsé Nináhálééh (Bird Monster), Tsédahódzííłtálii (Monster that Kicked People off the Cliff), Biináá'yee'agháanii (Monster that Kills with His Eyes), and others roamed the world.

The twins wanted a weapon; it had the appearance of a bow and arrow hanging over the north door of the father's home. The Sun was hesitant to give them the weapon since some of the monsters were also his children. But eventually he gave them the weapon; lightning. The twins also received body armor made of flint. The older brother was dressed in dark flint, while the younger was dressed in blue. The Sun also named the twins as the Diné peoples know them, Naayéé' Neezghání and Tó Bájísh Chíní. The Sun gave Monster Slayer atsiniltł'ish k'aa' (lightning that strikes crooked) and Child Born of Water hatsoo'algha k'aa' (lightning that flashes straight). The Sun told them how to kill Yé'iitsoh and requested a tail feather from Yé'iitsoh's headdress. The Sun gave one last instruction: the older brother was to kill the monsters while the younger brother watched a special firebrand stick to monitor how the older brother was progressing. If the older brother was in trouble, the younger brother could help, and only then.

The twins started their search for the monsters. The first monster they determined to kill was Yé'iitsoh. Yé'iitsoh lived near a hot spring. The twins waited for him to return home. They saw each other. Yé'iitsoh shot four arrows at the twins, but with the help of the magic eagle feathers they moved out of the path of the arrows. The twins shot back, first with a blinding flash of lightning, but Yé'iitsoh remained standing and did not fall. Then, the twins threw flint knives, and when the last weapon hit the monster, he fell with a terrible noise shaking the earth. Blood flowed out of the monster, and the twins prevented the blood from coming back together; Yé'iitsoh could have come back to life if the blood came together. The twins collected the tail feather and Yé'iitsoh's skull for the Sun. They returned home to their mother and told her of their accomplishment. At first, Changing Woman did not believe her sons; eventually, she realized it.

Monster Slayer went out alone to search for the other monsters after a short period of rest. He came into contact with Tsédahódzíiłtáłii at a place call Wild Horse Mesa, near present-day Mesa Verde, Colorado. The monster appeared in human form, and he looked pleasant and harmless. He lay beside a narrow path along the cliff in the shade. Monster Slayer asked if he could pass, and Tsédahódzíiłtáłii said yes. Monster Slayer pretended to take a step, but quickly drew back when the monster tried to kick him off the cliff with his foot. Four times Monster Slayer attempted to take a step, and four times the monster missed. Then Monster Slayer threw his knife at the monster and killed him. The monster's hair was embedded into the rock formation, and Monster Slayer had to cut the hair so the body could fall off the cliff.

Next, Monster Slayer went after Déélgééd. The Horned Monster had excellent eyesight, charged people, and ate people after it killed them. Monster Slayer tried to sneak up on Horned Monster, but he could not. He almost gave up when na'azisi (gopher) asked what he was doing. Monster Slayer told gopher he was trying to get as close as possible to Déélgééd to kill it. Gopher agreed to help him and began to dig a tunnel underneath the monster to where the heart was and began to chew off the hair covering the monster's heart. Then, Monster Slayer used his lightning arrow to strike the Horned Monster. He killed it. Monster Slayer returned home to tell his mother and brother he killed Déélgééd and Tsédahódzíiłtáłii.

After resting for a while, Monster Slayer set off to kill Tsé Nináhálééh. The giant killer bird and his family lived on top of Shiprock. Monster Slayer camouflaged himself by wearing hide skin and a part of the horn itself from Déélgééd, and he also placed two sacred feathers under his arms. He walked around Shiprock until the Monster Bird picked him up. Tsé Nináhálééh dropped him into the nest. Tsé Nináhálééh's children almost ate him. The children cried, but Monster Slayer told them to be quiet and he would not hurt them. He asked the children when their father would return, and the children responded their father would return when male rain fell. Later, male rain fell, and Tsé Nináhálééh returned home.

Monster Slayer killed Tsé Nináhálééh with his lightning arrow. Later female rain fell, and he killed the mother. Monster Slayer did not kill the two children, but told them to live good lives unlike their parents. The two bird children would later help Diné peoples. The older bird child became atsá (eagle) and the younger na'ashjaa' (owl). The two children flew away, but Monster Slayer needed to find a way to get down from the nest atop Tsé Bit'a'í (Rock with Wings). Monster Slayer saw an old woman below. He yelled down to her to help him. She was afraid at first, but realized it was Monster Slayer. Na'ashjé'ii 'Asdzáá was the old woman. Monster Slayer gave her the feathers from the wings and the tail of the Monster Bird to thank her for her help. Monster Slayer returned home and, with his brother's help, killed the remaining monsters.

The brothers returned home after killing all the monsters. They rested when they saw in the distance red smoke. They traveled to the smoke and found a hole in the earth. They looked inside and found several monsters resting. They quickly entered the place and attempted to kill them. Dichin Hastiih (Hunger), Tę'é'į Hastiih (Poverty), Bił Hastiih (Sleep), Yaa' Hastiih (Lice Man), and Sá (Old Age) were hiding. The twins were ready to kill them all when each monster pleaded for their existence. Dichin Hastiih argued that, without it, people would eat one meal forever, but when people were hungry they would eat and taste new foods. The twins agreed to spare hunger's life. Tę'é'į Hastiih argued that, without it, old things would not wear out, and new things would not be made. The twins spared poverty's life. Bił Hastiih, Yaa' Hastiih, and Sá also argued for their existence, and the twins spared their lives. All exist to this day.

After leaving the hole, the twins climbed the sacred mountains and searched in all four directions for other monsters, but they found none. They decided no other monsters existed. They returned home to Dził Ná'oodiłii (Huerfano Mountain). Monster Slayer took off his armor and laid down his weapons, their father visited them to take back the weapons. The sons returned all the weapons except for the sunray arrow and the sunray as a means to travel.

After staying a while at home, the twins decided to go visit their father again.[2] The twins asked for all the gifts they saw in their first visit, but their father said they asked for too much. Eventually, their father agreed to give all the gifts to his sons, but he wanted something in return. He wanted to destroy all those who lived in houses. After much consideration, the twins agreed to the offer. Jóhonaa'éí gave his sons obsidian; turquoise; abalone; white shell; horses; elk; antelopes; porcupines; deer; rabbits; white, blue, yellow, and black corn; striped and varicolored corn; other plants; corn pollen; and small birds. The twins also received rainbow, zigzag lightning, sunray, mirages, male and female rain, and dark and white mists. The twins returned home with the gifts. Meanwhile, four days before their father came to destroy all those living in houses, First Man, First Woman, and all of the people gathered up male and female essences and pairs of all living things to protect them from Jóhonaa'éí's destruction. On the fourth day, the Sun flooded the Earth destroying much of it. After a period of time, the flood receded.

Afterwards, Monster Slayer was distressed and lacked energy. He began to experience psychological problems as a result of taking Yé'iitsoh's skull.[3] The people meet to discuss how to help Monster Slayer. From this meeting, a new ceremony was created. The ceremony was called Monster Slayer Way. Building upon Monster Slayer Way, the Enemy Way ceremony known as 'Anaa'ji was created. Now, all peoples who come into contact with an enemy or illness must go through this ceremony to cleanse and protect themselves.

Several core values came from the stories of Changing Woman and her twin sons. For instance, the twins took responsibility for their actions. Monster Slayer and Child Born of Water wanted to protect the people from the monsters. Though they were afraid to confront these horrible monsters, they were triumphant. The twin sons were independent with a strong sense of identity acquired from their mother and extended family.

The twins epitomize the ideal image of a Diné man. A Diné man must be smart, he cannot be afraid of responsibility, and he must protect his family and the people. The twins are the first Diné protectors. Diné protectors are the strongest individuals in the community. They work for the people and not themselves. Monster Slayer and Child Born of Water were strong individuals who fought and killed monsters to protect their mother, First Man, First Woman, and all entities living in the world. Naayéé'Neezghání and Tó Bájísh Chíní set parameters for Diné masculinities.

Pre-European Invasion and the Spanish/Mexican Era

Diné men lived with their spouses' extended and clan families. They helped their families. Prior to the Spanish conquistadors' arrival to the Southwest,

Diné men served the community as protectors. Tiana Bighorse explained what being a protector means in Diné:

> When Mr. Bighorse is a boy, he goes with his father. His father teaches everything that a boy should do to become a man. And what he shouldn't do. And his father tells him, "You will be brave and be a warrior someday." In Navajo, a warrior means someone who can get through the snowstorm when no one else can. In Navajo, a warrior is the one that doesn't get the flu when everyone else does—the only one walking around, making a fire for the sick, giving them medicine, feeding them food, making them strong to fight the flu. In Navajo, a warrior is the one who can use words so everyone knows they are part of the same family. In Navajo, a warrior says what is in the people's hearts. Talks about what the land means to them. Brings them together to fight for it.[4]

Protectors thought of their family and relatives first; they were strong individuals. Diné men lived with their wife's family and made all possible efforts to ensure the survival of the extended family. Most of the daily activities included finding and fetching water, collecting firewood, finding and hunting game, maintaining the crops, teaching the child, and protecting the wife and extended family. Most Diné men did not spend much time away from their extended families. At times, some men visited their own biological parents, but for the most part they were with their wives' extended families. Men and women practiced an egalitarian and autonomous relationship. They integrated their work roles. Gender equity was a critical aspect of social life. Both men's and women's economic contributions were equally valuable.

Diné men served as the major communication link between the family and other peoples. Different clan groups and the surrounding Native communities established trading networks particularly with the Pueblos. Based on these interactions, Diné families incorporated elements of other native cultures they felt benefited their way of life.[5] For instance, they traded turquoise and other minerals for corn and other foods.

Both Diné men and women participated in the political system. Many of the heads or leaders of the extended and clan families were men, although a significant number were women, too. These leaders were called naat'áanii (planner). They met every two or four years to discuss pertinent issues. This gathering assembly was the naachid.[6] Men in leadership positions lived ethical and respectful lives. They were examples for the rest of the community, which relied on these individuals to make good decisions. If a leader did wrong, then the people let him/her know and, if necessary, removed him/her from the position. Naat'áaniis were supposed to follow the examples of the Holy People and the twins.

Diné men understood their role in life and in the extended and clan families. Not all of the men supported their families; some were selfish individuals who took advantage of people. Usually, these selfish men roamed by themselves. Overall, most men made sure their families were prosperous and happy. They were responsible, respectful, hospitable, knowledgeable, and healthy men who lived for the extended family. They advocated subsistence, self-sufficiency, respect, love, and humility to all.

Beginning in the seventeenth and continuing into the nineteenth century, the Spanish and Mexican ways impacted Diné way of life. A significant cultural impact was the introduction of livestock—sheep, goats, and horses. It is important to note, according to the creation narratives, Jóhonaa'éí introduced sheep to the people.

The Spanish and Mexican era contributed to new roles and responsibilities for Diné men—sheepherder and horse rider. While the men continued to live a subsistence lifestyle during this period (1540-1846), warfare, sheep herding, and the horse affected how Diné men interacted with Diné women; with other Native peoples such as the Pueblos, Comanches, and Utes; and with the Spanish and Mexican peoples. Warfare increased with the Pueblos, Comanches, Utes, Spanish, Mexicans, and New Mexicans because of the need to rescue family members.[7] The horse allowed Diné men to move more frequently and away from the family for extended periods of time. Diné men adapted very well to using the horse for trading, warfare, and travel.[8] The horse raised men's economic capacity, social status, ambition, and dependability. Diné men with horses ventured out to find food, trade, and interacted with more peoples. Diné masculinities became linked with how men maintained and cared for their horses.[9] Diné men who had horses and took care of them showed responsibility and status.

Uncles and grandmothers arranged marriages between Diné men and women, and a dowry consisting of horses was required. Diné men needed horses to increase economic capacity, social status, and dependability in the eyes of the people. A Diné man with no horses or other livestock in many cases had low status.[10] He needed to demonstrate to his future wife and her family he was dependable and capable of providing for the family.[11]

Raising sheep also shaped Diné communities. Sheep furnished security, which was an integral part of one's identity, and influenced how Diné social groups organized.[12] The ownership of sheep helped move people to cooperation and have mutual interdependence with one another. Sheep herding was the main mechanism to teach the characteristics and values of Diné thought. Sheep herding helped teach the principles in the creation narratives such as responsibility, respect, love, hospitality, knowledge, and health. Boys and girls were responsible for the sheep and the sheep dogs. The family expected them to meet that responsibility.

Many Diné men accepted the role and responsibility of sheepherder with integrity, pride, and honesty. A Diné man was looked upon positively when he took care of the sheep like his own family.[13] The man was ensuring the prosperity of his family and community when he cared for the sheep. Diné communities viewed the man as responsible and dependable when he provided for the well-being of his family and had no concern for his own selfish wants. If he did not take responsibility, and if a wife took care of the husband, the man was considered poor and not truly a Diné man.[14]

Besides taking care of the sheep and learning how to use the horse effectively, warfare influenced Diné masculinities during this era. Spanish, Mexican, and New Mexican military conflicts occurred sporadically from 1540 to 1846. Diné men defended their families against the Spanish, Mexicans, New Mexicans, Comanches, and Utes. They fought fiercely in many hostile encounters. The hostile confrontations at times were successful for the people, however some ended in the capture or death of Diné men, women, and children. The Spanish captured individuals, mostly women and children, for the slave trade system established in the seventeenth century.[15] Conflicts with the Spanish usually were an attempt by family members or relatives to rescue their relatives.[16]

The sheep, horse, and warfare with the Spanish and Mexican peoples added new roles and responsibilities for Diné men, yet the original principles of sustenance, responsibility, respect, hospitality, knowledge, and health did not end with new technology and clashes with different peoples. Diné men, especially those that were intelligent, remained key members of the community. The men needed to know the stories, chants, and prayers, along with cultural knowledge to sustain life. They were considered men of good judgment and had the authority to discuss key political and religious matters. Diné men adapted to changing situations to enhance their status, but they did not forget their core values. They worked with women to ensure family survival. More changes began to take place with the American invasion and the people's internment at Bosque Redondo (Hwééldi).

American Invasion

From 1846 to 1863, conflicts between the American military and the Diné were frequent. Several treaties were signed by both parties to make peace, but all were broken. New Mexicans wanted the United States government to protect them and pressured federal officials to do so.

In the summer of 1863, US Army General James Carleton ordered Colonel Christopher "Kit" Carson to attack and punish Diné peoples. Carson employed Utes, various Pueblos, Hopis, and the Diné Anaai (Enemy Navajos) to help in his campaign. By the winter of 1863-64, thousands of Diné surrendered to Carson. Carson was very effective in carrying out a scorched earth policy to subdue and subjugate the people. From 1864 to 1866, Carson and the US military rounded up thousands of men, women, and children and forced them to march over three hundred miles to the Bosque Redondo prison camp in eastern New Mexico, near present-day Fort Sumner. From 1863 to 1866, nearly ten thousand Diné people marched to the Bosque Redondo prison camp. At the same time thousands were sent off to Fort Sumner, hundreds eluded capture and hid in the Grand Canyon or in the Navajo Mountain region or among various Pueblo villages with relatives. Those who escaped capture tried to live a life free from fear. They maintained aspects of their way of life, while at the same time remaining watchful for the possibility of an American attack. Some integrated into Pueblo villages.

Diné peoples suffered tremendously at Bosque Redondo. They know Bosque Redondo as Hwééldi, which means "people suffering." The land at Bosque Redondo could not sustain corn, and the nearby Pecos River was salty. Most of the people at the prison camp depended on food rations from the government, but the food was so foreign it made them weak and sick. In addition, the Comanches, Kiowas, Mexicans, and New Mexicans stole women and children from the camp to sell as slaves. Diseases ravaged the camp, and a thousand people died during the incarceration.[17] Even with the enormous suffering at Bosque Redondo, hataałiis prayed to keep the people strong and hopeful.

The US military did not allow the men to carry weapons. Many men at Bosque Redondo suffered greatly because of the experience and what they saw on a daily basis. They saw women and children suffer and die. Many men found it difficult to endure and accept. They did not want their families to suffer anymore, and they constantly begged their leaders and the US military to send them home to Diné Bikéyah (Diné land). Diné leaders Barboncito, Manuelito, Armijo, and Largo worked diligently to return the people to Diné Bikéyah.

In 1868, because of the enormous costs and the obvious failure in the eyes of government officials of Bosque Redondo, the US government sent General William T. Sherman and Colonel Samuel F. Tappan to rectify the situation and to negotiate a treaty with the Diné peoples. A treaty was signed on June 1, 1868 allowing the peoples to return home to Diné Bikéyah. The treaty stipulated Diné peoples could no longer "raid," and that they must stay within the reservation boundaries established by the US government.[18] The treaty also outlined the people could not oppose the building of a transcontinental railroad through their homeland. As well, the people agreed to send their children to government schools. The US government in return would provide seeds, farm equipment, and livestock.

The peoples left Fort Sumner on June 18, 1868. Over 7,300 people walked the thirty-five days to reach Fort Wingate, New Mexico. They stayed at Fort Wingate until January 1869. Livestock was not distributed until November 1869. Each man, woman, and child received two animals. Barboncito, one of the leaders who signed the Treaty of 1868, spoke of the importance of this livestock:

> Now you are beginning again. Take care of the sheep that have
> been given you, as you care for your own children. Never kill
> them for food. If you are hungry, go out after the wild animals
> and the wild plants. Or go without food, for you have done

that before. These few sheep must grow into flocks so that we, the people, can be as we once were.[19]

The impact Hwééldi had on the people was traumatic and life altering. Diné peoples began to see themselves as one large community, new traditions developed such as the usage of flour to make fry bread, men learned new trades such as silversmith, women used commercial yarn to help with weaving, and the people began to be exposed to American thought and Christian influences.[20] Diné men shifted their way of life to be more sedentary and to not fight. While they continued to protect their families, Hwééldi influenced Diné men for many decades.

American Era

Many Diné peoples were self-sufficient by the end of the nineteenth century. The US government added land beyond the treaty reservation boundaries to increase grazing areas for the rapid livestock growth. Sheep herding and livestock growth established a cultural, social, and economic foundation for Diné communities at the end of the nineteenth century. The population of the people increased. For most families, the pastoral lifeway was the main economic staple. Men supplemented their income. They searched for means to acquire money to buy American goods. A few families sent their children to boarding schools to acquire an American education, but many refused.

Many men lived by the ideals set forth by Monster Slayer and Child Born of Water prior to Hwééldi. For the next forty years (1868-1908), changes to male roles and responsibilities occurred. Diné men continued to protect and provide for their families. However, some men "goofed around." Frank Mitchell, a well-known Blessing Way singer, described his own father as one who "goofed around." He said in *Navajo Blessingway Singer: The Autobiography of Frank Mitchell, 1881-1967*:

> While I was growing up and learning all these things, my father was starting to run around wild. Sometimes he would not come home for a long time. He had many wives, I do not even know how many, but any young man with clothes and wealth had lots of women attracted to him at that time. My father was that way; he had children by other women in other places; he

had some in Round Rock and Wheatfields that I know of, and
he had plenty of horses. I had no occasion to listen to him in
my early years because he was never home.[21]

With any male group, some men will go their own way and live differently.
Frank Mitchell's father lived recklessly and wildly in the nineteenth century.
Mitchell goes on even further to state, "In those days, men were just out for
a good time. They never thought about providing anything like a permanent
home for their family. My father made no plans for the future of his children.
He always had a horse ready to take off on."[22]

Gambling was a favorite activity for Diné men. Frank Mitchell himself
talked about his gambling activities, hoping to acquire wealth but never did.
He described his affliction: "Every time we were off, we played cards. I got
a fever to play cards with them, and I did not know that there were a lot of
crooked tricksters who knew how to cheat... the wages that were paid me, I
lost as soon as I was paid."[23]

Mitchell, like other Diné men, found jobs with the railroad company and
became influenced by American attitudes, behaviors, values, and beliefs. At
the beginning of the twentieth century, Diné masculinities reflected the principles of responsibility, respect, wellness, courage, and hospitality, but changes
started to occur. Besides subsistence herding and farming, men supplemented
their family's income with wage labor.

Diné communities began a significant transition in the early twentieth century. Non-Navajos criticized the way Diné peoples raised their livestock. The
federal government and Christian denominations wanted more children to attend schools. Meanwhile, the people got sick with trachoma, tuberculosis, and
influenza. Diné language was still strong among the children, but American
ideas and beliefs began to infiltrate Diné thinking. For example, future Navajo
Tribal Chairman Jacob C. Morgan attended Hampton Institute in Virginia and
learned to play the violin. He believed an American education was the key to
a better future for Diné peoples and worked as a disciplinarian and teacher at
Crownpoint, New Mexico in 1914. He wanted Diné peoples to live better, and
he believed an American education could help.

Diné men learned several new behaviors such as robbing women of economic and political power, and domestic abuse. They saw how Euro-American men behaved toward women. On occasion, Euro-American men did not

discuss with women "male issues" such as politics and economics. Prior to the American invasion, domestic and child abuse were an aberration in Diné families. Patriarchy infiltrated Diné thought after the Long Walk. Egalitarian and autonomous gender relations changed.

Diné peoples started to accept Western cultural items and ideas to "better" their communities. Yet, the peoples still wanted to incorporate on their own terms and not other people's. Diné men willingly accepted Western ideas and innovations for the betterment of themselves and their families as long as they remained Diné. For instance, the peoples accepted the American concept of fairs. They saw an opportunity to celebrate community with fairs. Agricultural exhibits, rodeos, horse races, and the opportunity to gather to see family, friends, and relatives became part of the fair experience.

The first regional fair took place in Shiprock, New Mexico in 1909. Non-Navajo traders along with community peoples established fairs in other parts of the reservation later, but the fairs on the reservation became distinctly Diné, and many men participated. Almost all men in the early twentieth century still spoke the language, took care of the livestock, chopped firewood, told stories to their children and grandchildren, learned core songs and prayers, and made sure their families ate. Many men still lived by the ideals set forth by the twin protectors. In contrast, alcoholism, domestic violence, negative attitudes toward a Diné way of life, and child abuse began to increase in the twentieth century.

In 1923, the Department of Interior (DOI) established a "business" council, consisting of twelve delegates representing five Navajo agency towns to approve oil leases. The twelve delegates only met when Herbert J. Hagerman, special DOI commissioner to Diné peoples, was present to approve oil and other mineral leases. The first tribal council was organized and controlled by outsiders. It marked an important step toward a centralized government system for all Diné peoples.

All twelve council delegates were men, and for the next twenty years all delegates to follow were men. No woman has served as Navajo Tribal Council Chairman (1923-1989) or president (1990-present). American attitudes played a role in deciding who served on the original "business" council and subsequent councils. The DOI never thought to ask Diné women who should serve on the "business" council. They went directly to various Diné male leaders at the time and asked several to serve. Diné men learned to adopt American definitions of leadership. One criteria Diné communities accepted was the idea that men lead. Starting with the first "business" council, men took on more of the political leadership role and women were relegated to the background.

While the formation of the "business" council in 1923 institutionalized twentieth century Diné nationalism, the livestock reduction program proposed by the Bureau of Indian Affairs and Commissioner of Indian Affairs John Collier forever changed Diné way of life. Since the return of the peoples from Bosque Redondo in 1868, many people raised livestock and farmed. Diné peoples were self-sufficient, though at times life was hard. The political and social economy of the peoples from 1868 to the 1930s was based on farming and on raising livestock. Collier instituted the livestock reduction program to reduce the number of sheep and horses each family could own to prevent further soil erosion. Some non-Diné people, including those in the federal government, scrutinized Diné peoples for the way they grazed their livestock. Non-Diné scientists predicted the destruction of the soil on the reservation and nearby areas. Collier chose livestock reduction as a way to save the soil. He never fully consulted with the people on how to save the soil and protect the livestock; instead, he initiated a radical solution, the reduction of thousands of livestock by any means. Many families lost their self-sufficiency, and they suffered tremendously. Their livelihood was taken, again. Some Diné peoples started to search for wage labor jobs, and some moved away from the reservation.

Consequently, many Diné peoples disliked Collier, the federal government, and the tribal council, who supported the reduction plan. Council delegates supported the livestock reduction program, except for Jacob C. Morgan and his supporters. Morgan's resistance to the program got him elected as chairman of the council in 1938, but he found out it was not as easy to resist the program or the federal government. He only served four years.

More Diné men looked to work in border towns such as Gallup, New Mexico and Farmington, New Mexico and places further away from the reservation. Urban migration continued into the 1970s.

World War II transformed America including accelerated changes in Diné communities. Over three thousand six hundred Diné men served in the US military, and nearly ten thousand Diné people worked in war-related industries.[24] Many Diné people fought to protect Diné Bikéyah and their way of life, even though they faced discrimination and racism at home. Even then, some men joined the US military to get away from the reservation. They wanted something to do besides sheep herding and farming, which no longer guaranteed a prosperous livelihood.

Even though thousands of Diné men fought to protect the United States in World War II, they recognized prejudice and discrimination existed at home. Some veterans refused to speak English because of the discrimination encountered in the military and elsewhere.[25] Men and women faced inequality in the work place and were denied the right to vote in the states of Arizona until 1948 and in New Mexico until 1962. The war affected every aspect of a Diné way of life. The peoples realized they were a part of the United States and did not live in isolation from the rest of America. More Diné parents began to send their children to schools to receive a formal Western education.

Diné peoples went through a huge transition phase from the end of World War II in 1945 through the 1970s. Education, health care, economic development, voting rights, religious freedom especially for Native American Church members, mineral development, and the changing economy transformed how men and women lived for the second half of the twentieth century. While many people still lived by the essential principles of responsibility, respect, hospitality, knowledge, and wellness, more men worked in wage labor jobs, and more children were in American schools.

Western education became the foremost priority for Diné peoples after World War II. Diné parents sent their children to boarding schools. The tribal council wanted the peoples to support themselves, and they felt the best way to do this was to acquire an American education. "Education is our greatest need," the Council declared in the 1940s. "There are no schools for over 14,000 of our children. Our people are now very poor. Our children must have a good education if they are to learn to support themselves."[26] Thousands of Diné children went to boarding schools and a "Special Navajo Program."[27] The "Special Navajo Program" was a federally funded vocational education program. Students would spend five years learning a vocational trade to help them live and work off the reservation. From 1946 to 1959, more than fifty thousand Diné students went through the special program at various off-reservation boarding schools.[28]

Thousands of young boys went to school and in most cases found work off the reservation. Many moved to cities in California, Arizona, New Mexico, Texas, Colorado, Illinois, and other places. Experiences at the boarding schools varied for each child, but the traumatic affect has remained for generations.

The traumatic affects from boarding schools continue. The experiences lead some men to alcoholism and depression. Some Diné men were grateful for their experiences at boarding schools however, many boys did not learn nor respect the stories of Naayéé' Neezghání and Tó Bájísh Chíní.

Another impact of government boarding schools was the prohibition of tribal languages. Some Diné people felt speaking English helped to better their lives. These schools' English focused curriculum began the process of fewer children learning to speak Diné and knowing the stories of their peoples. The need to live in the American world negated Diné thought that their parents, grandparents, and great-grandparents learned as children. During the 1950s, many Diné peoples acculturated to American values, beliefs, and attitudes. More and more men, from their perception, began to leave the reservation to "get away" from the problems of the reservation and the "backwards" way of life.

By the 1950s, the tribal government was seen by most, if not all Diné, as representative of Diné peoples. The tribal council chairman was the head official. In 1962, Raymond Nakai was elected chairman, and his main platform was to push for greater acculturation into American society. He called for educational achievement, economic development, improving relations with the federal government and surrounding states, and the need for religious tolerance, particularly, the acceptance of the Native American Church on the reservation.

Subsequent Chairman Peter MacDonald made bold goals for the people in 1971. He sets forth three primary objectives for his administration: "First, what is rightfully ours, we must protect; what is rightfully due us we must claim. Second, what we depend on from others, we must replace with the labor of our own hands and the skills of our own people. Third, what we do not have, we must bring into being. We must create for ourselves."[29] MacDonald and many Diné peoples saw the opportunity to fully succeed in American society. The core principles of sustenance, courage, responsibility, respect, hospitality, knowledge, and wellness were lessening with more Diné peoples wanting to live an American lifestyle.

The tribal council sought ways to develop the economy on the reservation, and in many cases the decisions the council made negatively affected Diné men and women. For example, the council allowed Kerr-McGee and Vanadium Corporation of America to establish uranium mines on the Navajo reservation in the 1950s.[30] The companies and the federal government never told the council or the men who worked in these mines the dangers of uranium. Hundreds of men worked for Kerr-McGee in uranium mines near Shiprock from 1952 to 1963.[31] Hundreds died later from lung cancer.[32] The tribal council approved other mineral development projects in the 1960s to generate revenue. The approval of Peabody Coal Company to mine Black Mesa, and to use precious underground water to transport the coal to the Mojave generating power plant in Nevada, lead to the removal of thousands of families from their homelands as well as hundreds of Hopis. Only a few hundred Diné men found work with Peabody.

In the 1970s and 1980s, Diné communities acculturated rapidly to American attitudes and values. The transition to live in mainstream America and speak English was more prominent. The need to find wage labor forced men and women to move to agency towns like Shiprock, Crownpoint, Kayenta, Tuba City, and border towns such as Flagstaff and Winslow, Arizona. Many families moved from the rural areas of the reservation to agency towns, border towns, and cities such as Los Angeles, Phoenix, and Albuquerque. This pattern of urban growth, coupled with nearby primary and secondary school education, altered Navajo life.[33] Soon, fewer men spoke the Diné language, and more adopted Christianity as their primary religion and spirituality. Herding sheep and planting crops dwindled.

The consequences of change for some men become detrimental. Some became alcoholics and criminals. For instance, a participant in Stephen J. Kunitz and Jerrold E. Levy's study in *Drinking, Conduct Disorder, and Social Change: Navajo Experiences* described his former drinking pattern as a "weekend warrior" where he drank "pretty heavy" on weekends with his friends. Heavy drinking with friends was a pattern for young Diné men in the 1970s and 1980s as mobility increased on and off the reservation. According to Kunitz and Levy, this pattern influenced the changing nature of Diné communities increasing urbanization and education. This change created a young Diné culture of "binge drinking" beginning in the 1970s and continuing to this day. According to Martin D. Topper, young men drank to be a part of a socially cohesive unit and to escape daily problems. Young boys also drank to "show off" their manhood.[34] Young men learned to maintain a particular definition of manhood through drinking. The frustrations and stresses drove many young men to drink. Some young men also joined gangs in the 1970s.[35] Gangs started to influence Diné boys beginning in the 1970s, and for the past forty years numerous gangs have formed on the reservation impacting some young Diné men.[36]

For many young men, the fundamental principles of sustenance, responsibility, respect, hospitality, knowledge, and wellness, which their ancestors learned at a young age, declined with the waning of the pastoral economy and greater participation in the American school system and American lifestyle. Sporadic contact with relatives and a Diné way of life experienced by their parents and grandparents lead some Diné men to a marginalize life vastly different and foreign.

Conclusion

Diné men and peoples are interconnected with the United States. Some men have had a difficult time adjusting to this lifestyle. Many still work in low paying jobs. Some have earned college degrees, but more Diné women graduate from college than men.[37] Most men either go to work right after high school or join the US military to access economic opportunities.

While the Diné way of life has changed, Diné communities continue. Some men continue to provide and protect for their families. Some schools on the reservation teach Diné history, culture, and language. Many people take pride in being Diné. Basketball and rodeo are now "traditional" games for the people.[38] Many people tell their children to be successful in life, and to never forget they are Diné. Diné peoples have adapted to different situations and changing environments, which have steered them to live a different way of life from their ancestors.

Diné men live individualistic lives, like most, if not all Americans. Many young men have different upbringings from their grandfathers or great-grandfathers. Some struggle with alcoholism or poverty or some other socioeconomic challenge. Some are in the military to make a better future for themselves or their families. Some work hard to provide for themselves or for their families. Some do not have jobs, and some are in prison. Some have college degrees and are professionals. Some are learning to become hataałiis. Some still herd livestock. Some create art, or silversmith. Some take care of relatives. Some are womanizers. Some are homeless. All of these roles and experiences represent Diné masculinities in the twenty-first century.

Diné masculinities have changed, and the historical principles Naayéé' Neezghání and Tó Bájísh Chíní lived by have minimized. In fact, some men do not know these principles, while others do, but choose not to live by them, though some do live by these values. New principles influence Diné men. One principle Diné men follow is the American perspective on what it means to be a man. Diné men display their masculinities by "doing manly things" based on American attitudes, behaviors, and values. Some Diné men do not validate their masculinities on the principles of Naayéé' Neezghání and Tó Bájísh Chíní, but rather emulate what American men say and do. Some Diné men view the American perspective of what it means to be a man as homogenous, singular, and uncomplicated yet numerous studies show American masculinity is not singular but plural, multiple, and as diverse as any human population on the planet.

4
Foundational Image of Diné Masculinities

What establishes a Diné man? The answer lies within each individual Diné man and the Diné peoples. History, matrix, and a people's way of life established Diné masculinities. The foundational image of a Diné man supplies an understanding of Diné masculinities.

While this chapter explores the foundational image of a Diné man, he is incomplete without his opposite, a Diné woman. This foundational image applies to Diné women as well. Girls participate in their own puberty ceremonies and have their own distinct roles and responsibilities. To fully comprehend what establishes Diné masculinities, an individual will need to have an understanding of Diné thought. Fully understanding Diné thought can only occur with Diné language comprehension and learning this knowledge within the confines of Diné Bikéyah. The description in this chapter is only touching the surface for the non-Diné audience. Diné thought equates to iiná. While *worldview* and *matrix* are Western terms to help people understand the approaches to living, iiná is a clear vision and purpose of what the Holy People intended for Diné peoples.

The descriptions and discussions on a fundamental Diné male image do not necessarily apply to all Diné men. However, they show the knowledge Diné men learn in their development from infanthood to elderhood. This chapter is not designed to critique Diné men because each Diné man is distinct and his experiences valid. Those distinctions along with varied experiences represent Diné masculinities.

Image Foundation

Each man and woman is made up of four distinct components: spiritual, common, social, and physical. Each component represents a quadrant of a human's image. To understand a more detailed description of each component, one must discuss the images with a hataałii in the Diné language. The following paragraphs are a general and Western description of each component.

The first image of a man is spiritual. It is located in the East and is represented by the Holy entities of Talking God, Dawn Boy, and Dawn Girl. This image explains a man's spiritual appearance. Men and women are born of this image. From this image, humans experience the force of all universal laws in nature. The spiritual image helps people experience positive energy, happiness, and laughter. With this image, people enjoy life. People develop a good attitude and behavior. People's motivation gains the necessary energy to direct their needs and desires in life. Human beings need to understand this energy in order to control it. This image can direct you toward the positive interests you have as a human being. Diné men and women develop good emotions and thoughts about themselves. People's outlook on life and the approach they take derives from a positive spiritual image.

The second image of a man is common or conventional. It is located in the South and is represented by Talking God, Blue Twilight Boy, and Blue Twilight Girl. It represents the "normal" way people feel and act. People can develop good or bad common images. While the spiritual image relates to the abstract, the common focuses on how men and women present themselves to people. The common image symbolizes the way a person is viewed by the world. It is tangible and visible. People's childhood, belief system, and lifestyle create the common image. The different life experiences will shape and mold people's common image and life pattern.

The third image of a man is social. It is located in the West and is represented by Second Talking God, Yellow Evening Boy, and Yellow Evening Girl. The social image concerns each person's outlook on life within the framework of Diné cultural teachings. People's interactions with all creations of the world such as the mountains, rivers, seasons, animals, plants, beliefs, and values dictate the social image. A person learns how to interact with other humans and nonhumans. From this interaction, Diné individuals comprehend their own personality. All of this understanding takes place within Diné thought.

Diné peoples learn about life from the cultural teachings, stories, and prayers. For instance, K'é and K'éí represent the relationship and clanship systems for the people to know and understand their relations. K'é and K'éí establishes a family network. It instills in all Diné family support and protection in interacting with life's complexities. In Diné thought, K'é teaches the people that all creations in the world are intertwined with one another, and no one is alone.

The social image is a developing and continuing process; with each new interaction, men and women continuously develop the social image. Men and women at times will have conflicts with their own social images, so each needs to be careful. A balance must be achieved with the social image; if not, men and women can suffer and venture into areas harmful for human beings. The social image is the most vulnerable of all the images, yet it establishes the values humans follow in life.

The fourth image of a man is the physical. It is located in the North and is represented by the Second Talking God, Folding Darkness Boy, and Folding Darkness Girl. When the Holy People came into this world, the physical image of the people was formed in darkness. A person's physical image focuses on the outside appearance, the way a person looks, and the way human physical features are put together. Human beings do not control the physical image. The other three images are considered more important. The physical features should not be a significant concern for people if they understand the other three images. If Diné men and women accept their physical appearance, they will understand their own foundation. The physical aspects of men and women represent the behaviors and attitudes each lives by on a daily basis.

Each individual Diné person consists of the four images. The Diyin Dine'é designed these components to help Diné peoples understand themselves and their personhood. These images establish each man and woman.

Iiná: Way of Life

When the Diyin Dine'é left this world, Diné peoples learned the songs, prayers, and the intricacies of numerous ceremonies and how to live as a Diné man and woman.[1] In turn, grandmothers, grandfathers, mothers, fathers, aunts, uncles, and extended family members teach their grandchildren, children, nephews, and nieces how to live as a hastiin and a 'asdzą́ą́n. This living process is referred to as iiná and is the framework for a human. This description is incomplete without the proper stories and cultural teachings from a hataałii and learned within the confines of Diné Bikéyah. It is important to note these paragraphs are not of a comprehensive nature of a Diné way of life. This description, however, will provide a good starting point for discussion and analysis.

In order to grasp the complexities of iiná, a Diné way of life will be organized into seven zones. The first zone teaches Diné men and women to live in symmetry and harmony. Eight components make up this first zone. In order for men and women to achieve balance and harmony, they must have bi'oodla (belief), show faith, provide protection, develop mental and physical skills, know the universal laws, know the deities, know the good and bad elements in life, and live off the land through farming and ranching.

First, bi'oodla is an offering. Offerings are given on a daily basis, for specific rituals and ceremonies, during the seasons, and in emergencies. Most often, an offering is given in the form of tádídíín (corn pollen) to Mother Earth. A prayer is usually said in the Diné language. Diné are instructed to get up before sunrise each morning and run to the East to the rising sun. He or she runs in a specific pattern and offers the new day and Mother Earth tádídíín. The offering and prayer helps the individual and the community with prosperity, good health, and the necessary protection to walk in this world. These offerings teach Diné men the value of reciprocity, respect, and love for all living things on the Earth and in the universe.

Second, Diné men and women display their faith by way of prayers, songs, and participating in ceremonies. During a specific ceremony such as Hózhǫ́ǫ́jí (Blessing Way) men and women participate to promote good will, healthy living, and happiness for the patient and all participants who attend the ceremony. This ceremony is the backbone of all Diné ceremonies.

Third, prayers, songs, and ceremonial participations are the blueprints for protection of the individual and the community. Many entities and energies can cause great harm to people, and protections are needed to ensure the safety and wellbeing of the individual and community. So, certain protocols and rules must be followed, and prayers to the Diyin Dine'é are required.

Fourth, men and women must develop their mental and physical skills. Physical abilities are trained and strengthened by running, horseback riding, dancing, singing, and being physically active. Mental abilities are also trained and strengthened through thinking, planning, learning, memorizing, analyzing, and reflecting. These abilities develop strong and healthy Diné men and women.

Fifth, men and women are taught early in life the protocols and rules for living. Parents teach their children about the geography of the area, the limitations of curiosity, and the restrictions to exploration. Boys and girls are also taught how to interact with harmful areas in life.

Sixth, the children are told of the most common of the Diyin Dine'é such as Talking God, Changing Woman, White Corn Boy, Yellow Corn Girl, and others. Diné boys and girls also learn moral and ethical lessons in life. They are instructed to strive for the ideal and to be careful regarding life's traps. Those ideal means are what Diné men strive for in their lives to this day.

Seventh, along with learning about the Diyin Dine'é, Diné children learn about the necessity of bad elements. They learn life has both positive and negative elements. They also learn about the origin and purpose of the bad elements. While people are told not to discuss bad elements in public, they understand they are interwoven with good qualities in life.

Eighth, farming and ranching teaches boys and girls how to make a living and to survive in this world and to protect themselves against adverse conditions. Men and women learn how to plant, when to plant, what to plant, how to maintain the crops, how to water, how to harvest, how to hunt, how to butcher sheep, how to create and use the tools necessary for farming and ranching, and how to store and prepare food. All eight components of this first zone teach Diné men and women the properties of prosperity and happiness and how to live in balance with the Earth and the universe.

The second zone teaches Diné men and women the history of the people. The people learn by oral tradition. Both men and women learn the critical stories and experiences of the ancestors. This knowledge establishes the attitudes, behaviors, beliefs, values, and standards in Diné thought. Information is learned and passed down to children and the younger generations.

Certain responsibilities for men include teaching children to sing, modeling proper behavior, and developing children's physical activity. Women teach the children how to pray, how to dress, the history of their four clans, and how to maintain a proper diet.[2] The primary purpose of the cultural teachings is to establish a person's grounding.

Key entities in the creation narratives furnish children with an understanding of why ceremonies, songs, and prayers are conducted in a structured manner. For example, the twin protectors' stories teach courage, responsibility, endurance, wellness, love, and knowledge.

The third zone covers the strategies and matrices in Diné thought. This zone is the most humanizing and detailed aspect of iiná and is linked to SNBH. SNBH is the natural order of all life. Diné educator Herbert John Benally describes SNBH as:

> The sacred words Sa'ah Naagháí Bik'eh Hózhǫǫn represent a combination of separate male and female concepts. The first concept, Sa'ah Naagháí, is defined as "indestructible and eternal being." It is male and exhibits male-like qualities. The second concept, Bik'eh Hózhǫǫn, is defined as "the director and cause of all that is good." It is female and exhibits female-like qualities. The two concepts do not operate apart, but are complements to and halves of each other.[3]

SNBH is experienced and better understood within the confines of Diné Bikéyah.

SNBH is the epistemological base in a Diné matrix. SNBH metaphorically represents the creators of this world. SNBH came from the medicine bundles of First Man and are the parents to 'Asdzą́ą́ Nádleehé.[4] The sacred words represent a combination of separate male and female principles. Both principles are complements and halves to each other and never operate alone. Anthropologist Gary Witherspoon describes these complements:

> Sa'ah Naagháí and Bik'eh Hózhǫǫn represent the underlying dynamic, holistic asymmetry of the universe. Sa'ah Naagháí is the inner form of Bik'eh Hózhǫǫn, which is the outer form of Sa'ah Naagháí. Sa'ah Naagháí is the static dimension of the universe while Bik'eh Hózhǫǫn is the active dimension. Sa'ah Naagháí is the thought of the universe, while Bik'eh Hózhǫǫn is its speech or voice. The dynamic, fertile, and omnipotent union of these two dimensions of the universe is what produces hózhǫ.[5]

SNBH is the foundational system of the people and entails the concept of good and bad.[6]

In a Diné matrix, everything in the cosmos is composed of both male and female pairs. The interaction of the pairs creates life and represents the active nature of the universe. SNBH is life force. Diné men and women strive to live in perfect balance and symmetry between the pair. In walking this fine line, one must partake of things in moderation. Moderation is key, since too much of the positive or negative is harmful.[7] The principles of this pair is significant in Diné thought. The human body is symmetrical, and the cosmos replicates this symmetry such as the two constellations Náhookǫs bika'ii (Big Dipper), which is male, and Náhookǫs bi'aadii (Cassiopeia), which is female. The Diné names translate as the "male one who revolves" and the "female one who re-volves," respectively.[8] SNBH is everywhere on Earth and in the universe. The right side of the human body is female, and the left side is male. The brain is also divided along male and female lines. Diné thought conceptualizes life in pairs, male and female.

Along with symmetry, men and women learn the life stage cycle. The cycle depicts the stages in life one enters and the principles one learns and the responsibilities one has in each stage. The properties of the cardinal di-rections are paired with each life stage.[9] East (ha'a'aah) represents birth, the spring season, and the beginning of the thinking process (nitsáhákees). South (shádi'ááh) represents adolescence, the summer season, and the planning pro-cess (nahat'á). West ('e'e'aah) represents adulthood, the fall season, and the living process (iiná). North (náhookǫs) represents old age, the winter season, and the reflecting process (siihasin). Other principles and elements are in each direction. The hogan (home) as well represents the life stage cycle. The en-trance to the hogan always faces east. It represents dawn and the birth of each human being. This direction possesses clearly established standards for guid-ance in decision-making. The third zone encompasses the most comprehensive view of iiná.

The fourth zone represents the four basic elements in life: fire, water, air, and Earth. Each element and its purpose are told to men when they enter the táchéii (sweathouse).[10] In the táchéii, the men sing songs and share stories. Diné men learn about the first sweathouse assembled by the Diyin Dine'é upon entering this world. In the sweathouse, men sing twenty-four songs, discuss issues, and devel-op plans. The sweathouse has four purposes: purification, hygiene, planning, and sharing stories.[11] Men learn how to think, talk, plan, and implement in the táchéii. For instance, men will discuss an issue, come up with how to deal with it, and then put it into action.

The fifth zone is the relationship and clanship systems. In Diné communities, the relationship system is known as K'é, and the clanship system is known as K'éí. It is a living system designed to help Diné men and women know their relations in the world and the universe, their lineage, and their families. Clans function as a social grouping mechanism. When one is born, the clan of the mother is automatically the clan of the child whether male or female. The father's clan becomes the one the child is "born for." Everyone from his/her father's clan is related, so the person will have many uncles, aunts, and cousins on both sides of the family.

K'éí creates a family network for each person, and he or she will have several father and mother figures, and cousins will become brothers and sisters. For instance, the person's older brother, on the maternal side of the family, is called shínaaí, and older sister is shádi. Those terms apply as well to cousins on the maternal side of the individual's family. Each Diné man and woman has four clans: mother, father, maternal grandfather, and paternal grandfather. He or she learns the history of all four clans and related clans. Relationship terminologies create a familial community across hundreds of individuals.[12]

The sixth zone is a career or trade. Diné men learn certain trades such as farming, herding livestock, silversmithing, and hunting, while women learn weaving, cooking, farming, and herding livestock. By the age of twelve, a young man or young woman starts on their own career or trade path. A career contributes to an adult identity.

The final zone is language. Diné bizaad, or Diné language, is a necessity, because without language, all areas cannot be communicated and comprehended. Some Diné individuals spoke several different languages long ago, but many in the twenty-first century are fluent only in the English and Diné languages. Consequently, language changes with the people as new situations develop while older ones disappear. Language is core to Diné knowledge. Without language, the initial teachings, prayers, songs, and stories are altered. Language orients and directs Diné continuance.

All seven zones contribute to iiná. Each area is intertwined with every other, and both boys and girls learn each component. A completed education occurs when men and women reach maturity. For most in historical Diné communities, maturity begins around the age of twelve when girls have their first menstrual period, and a boy's voice changes. A ceremony is conducted to initiate a girl to womanhood and a boy to manhood. A brief description of the puberty ceremony for boys follows.

Kinaadlá: Puberty Ceremony

'Asdzáá Nádleehé is the first Kinaaldá. Changing Woman's twin sons, Naayéé' Neezghání and Tó Bájísh Chíní, are the first boys to experience the male kinaaldá. The male kinaaldá is conducted far less than the female today.[13] One reason is that many people do not know how to conduct the male kinaaldá ceremony. Nonetheless, the male kinaaldá ceremony survives and continues. It has been adapted to present day living, yet the boys who partake in the ceremony still learn the main lesson: to acquire the necessary skills to live in this world and ensure the community's well-being.

The male kinaaldá is a two-part ceremony. Boys train prior to the ceremony, and as the boy transforms from child to adolescent his family and relatives prepare him for the ceremony and life. When a boy's voice changes, it is time for the boy to partake in the kinaaldá ceremony. The first part of the ceremony takes place over four days, and the oldest maternal uncle guides the ceremony. His maternal uncle prepares the sweat lodge and the herbs for the ceremony. The boy gets up early every day for the four-day ceremony to run to the East before dawn, and is given herbs to make him vomit to purify himself. The young boy spends a significant amount of time in the táchéii and learns cultural teachings.

Among some Diné peoples, the táchéii is viewed more specifically as the male initiation ceremony and it lasts one or four days depending on the family. Some believe taa' represents a communication breath line from Father Sky to men's inner selves and chéii means to rid the imbalances as a way to engage naayéé'ijí (problems/challenges) situations in life.

Oscar Tso in Maureen Trudelle Schwarz's *Molded in the Image of Changing Woman: Navajo Views on the Human Body and Personhood* describes his puberty ceremony:

> They built a sweat for me, and they talked to me about my responsibilities as a man. And then, what I need to do to take care of myself. They talked about how I should be when I get

married. What should I know and how I should be towards a woman, because I have a mother, I have sisters. And I have to have respect for my mother, my sisters and then have that same respect for a woman that I will marry. And then all the daughters that I will have, or granddaughters that I will have. So, those kinds of things are explained to you. And then about how you need to keep yourself real strong, try to stay with one woman for a long time, you know. Have one set of children. And they can really preach, you know, and talk to you about a lot of things. And those are some things that are explained to boys. And then, how you have to be strong, what kind of herbs you have to take from time to time to purify and cleanse your body. To keep your mind and body strong, and have a sense of purpose as you go about living this life. So, I had the sweat done for me, as well as the Beauty Way, the Hoozhonee done for me.[14]

Oscar and other boys who participate in the sweat learn confidential teachings, life's complexities, and sincerity with humor. Inside and outside of the táchéii, the boy is massaged, with the focus points being the joints to ensure he is physically strong. The first part of the ceremony takes place over four days, and each day the boy is given a sweat. He also runs during the heat of the day, around noon, and he is told to think and make plans during the morning hours of the day. He also learns parenting skills.[15]

The second part takes place a month later and is similar to the first part of the ceremony, with the addition of an Hózhǫǫjí ceremony. The ceremony is to protect the young man. Tobacco is used in the ceremony, and the purpose is to open and expand the mind of the young man. The ceremony derives from the Twin Protectors story. The Sun gave his twin sons tobacco to test whether or not they were his sons. After the twins smoked the tobacco, their father massaged them with the ashes. It is done the same way for a boy undergoing the puberty ceremony. Father Berard Haile documented the story of the twins and the tobacco test during his time spent with Diné peoples in the early twentieth century.

After that he called upon his children, the dawn children, to come to him. When they came to him, they were carrying something or other, suspended from a dawn cord. It seems that they were carrying a dawn ladle, a dawn bowl, and dawn pollen, when they approached the boys. With these things they set to work on them, rubbing them with dawn pollen, with sky blue pollen, and with evening twilight pollen. With darkness pollen they rubbed their hair. After that they began to shape them from their feet up, and made them look exactly as they themselves looked. Then, it seems, they took them to their home, where they dressed them in clothes, such as they themselves were wearing, in dawn shoes, dawn leggings, dawn garments, and dawn headbands. "There is still one trial left," the sun said. Crystal rocks were burning there and produced a great, crackling noise. He picked up a turquoise pipe, which he had, and used a white bead ram to poke around in it, then filled it with his tobacco [this was poison tobacco, but the twins survived with the help of an antidote]... After they had finished smoking they set the pipe down. "Isn't this a surprise, my sons, my children! It's true! You really are my children!" he said to them. The remaining tobacco ashes he shook out into his hand, then told them to place their feet together, which they did. He then spit upon the ashes, and set to work on the boys by pressing them with it, much as their brothers and sisters had previously done. As he did this he kept up this speech, "My children, Changing Woman's children, White Bead Woman's children, my children, have care not to ask something extraordinary of me, whatever your purpose in coming may be! Should I ask you, is it this or that, be satisfied, and do not ask for me, my children, please!" he was saying and pleading, while he pressed them.[16]

Tobacco is used in the male kinaaldá ceremony to this day, even though it is not used in all Hózhǫ́ǫ́jí ceremonies. After the ceremony is complete, a boy begins a new stage in his life as a young man (dinééh).

The young man learns the songs, prayers, and stories and receives an arrowhead, a sacred corn pollen bag, and a bow with arrows.[17] He learns how to hunt deer. All of this takes place when he is between the ages of twelve and fourteen. In a short amount of time, he will marry with the help of his family. Basically, two questions are asked of a future marriage partner: what are your clans and did the person go through a puberty ceremony? If the answer is yes to the second question, and the individuals are not related to each other, in many occasions a marriage is arranged. The young man and woman are now ready to start on their life journey as a new family.

The male and female puberty ceremony strengthens and guides a person's adult life and helps a man or woman live a long and prosperous life for him/herself and his/her family. Without the ceremony, a man does not begin to learn the necessary skills and knowledge to live a Diné way of life. The ceremony is an acknowledgement point in a person's life when learning and comprehending all areas of Diné knowledge.

Some non-Diné scholars viewed the lack of a male kinaaldá ceremony as a reason to think they were nonexistent. Gladys Reichard thought so:

> No particular moment makes the transition from boyhood to manhood. When the Navaho were even more mobile than they are now, the boy had to be trained for activities, which took him away from home—hunting, war and trading. Young boys then submitted to rigorous physical training for their self-protection… nowadays there is little formal training; consequently the boy's life goal is but vaguely defined.[18]

Reichard and other scholars observed the transformations Diné peoples were undergoing in the early twentieth century. Unfortunately, the male puberty ceremony was conducted far less. The trend continues although the male ceremony is recovering. The girl's ceremony is conducted more often and is better known. Among the men interviewed, only four went through a male kinaaldá. Some families are reviving the male puberty ceremony, but it remains far less frequently conducted than the girl's ceremony.

The girl's puberty ceremony derives from the transformation of Changing Woman into White Bead Woman or White Shell Woman. The Diyin Dine'é living on the Earth at the time performed the first kinaaldá ceremony. The ceremony was held at Ch'óol'į'į (Gobernador Knob). Certain procedures and protocols were formed at the first kinaaldá. At the end of the ceremony, Changing Woman was no longer a girl, but a woman. She gave birth to children. She is the mother of all Diné peoples.

All girls are Kinaaldá and personify White Bead Woman at the end of the ceremony. Numerous texts document the girls' kinaaldá ceremony (Franciscan Fathers 1910: 446; Reichard 1928:135-39; Wyman and Bailey 1943; Leighton and Kluckhohn 1947: 76-77; Keith 1964; Frisbie 1993[1967]; Roessel 1981:81-100; Begay 1983). Many Diné families plan in advance for this ceremony, purchasing, making, or borrowing all necessary materials and articles of attire. Family members also will dry corn and save husks from their fields, or buy the corn and husks. Relatives or friends will make a bé'ézhoo' (hairbrush), an'adistiin (set of stirring sticks), and other items necessary for the ceremony.

Many Diné families prepare diligently for a girl's puberty ceremony, yet preparation for a young boy is not done as much. Many young boys learn their role as young Diné men and future husbands, uncles, and elders from their ceremony. They also learn they must choose a career.

Roles/Responsibilities

Specific roles and responsibilities for Diné men and women helped their families and communities. Consequently, Diné women did not merely sit at home to wait for Diné men to bring home food. Both played integral roles in maintaining the home, the family, the clan, and the natural community. Men hunted, farmed, and worked with women to maintain life. Before Spanish, Mexican, and American influences, Diné men were hunters, farmers, hataałiis, teachers, storytellers, traders, and protectors. Diné families traded with other indigenous peoples and took on new items and ideas. Diné men along with the rest of the community incorporated certain traits, ideas, and tools to enhance iiná. For instance, Diné communities learned to plant chiles and other seeds Pueblo communities used.

Other roles and responsibilities developed with the Spanish, Mexican, and American invasions such as sheepherding and silversmithing. Diné men learned to create artistic items to trade or sell to traders, however this role did not fully support these men and their families. For many men, these roles supplemented other duties and responsibilities to their wives, children, relatives, and communities. Diné women would also adopt new items, such as certain fabrics and yarns into their weaving. Interactions with the Spanish, Mexican, and American peoples provided Diné men opportunities to expand their roles and responsibilities. Unfortunately, for some men they chose to focus only on what they could accomplish individually and not for their families, relatives, and communities. Some Diné men did think of their families, relatives, and communities while they earned money. However, they spent large amounts of time away from their families, homes, and communities. Diné masculinities became intermixed with wage labor and, in turn, affected a Diné way of life. Wage labor soon influenced how Diné men constructed and displayed their individual masculinity within a communal setting.

Conclusion

Diné men were hunters, farmers, teachers, storytellers, traders, protectors, sheepherders, and healers. They established masculinities through a spiritual, social, common, and physical image. A boy learned his responsibilities as a young man in the puberty ceremony and established a career. His opposite— a Diné woman help define a Diné man. Without Diné women, Diné men are incomplete. These women function through various female roles such as wife, mother, grandmother, sister, aunt, etc.

Diné men live the principles of iiná. Men strived to live a life based on SNBH. They learned the history of the people and deities, used the four basic elements to survive, learned their family's history and recognized their relatives, practiced cultural production, and spoke the Diné way (Dinék'ehjí yáłti). In the puberty ceremony, the young boy learns cultural teachings and life's complexities. He sings songs, prays, and listens to stories. He also receives an arrowhead, a sacred corn pollen bag, and a bow with arrows. The knowledge he learns frames his purpose and mission. The female kinaaldá is also conducted. A girl learns the skills and knowledge for her transformation into womanhood. Both boys and girls are given the structure necessary to understand their purpose and mission in life.

A Diné image is establish by the cultural knowledge and matrix of the people. This foundational image creates Diné masculinities as distinctly Diné, yet American thought influences how Diné men develop, display, and view their relations with Diné women, the Diyin Dine'é, and a Diné way of life.

5
Iiná: Diné Male Perspectives

I interviewed thirty Diné men between the ages of eighteen and seventy. These thirty individuals provide a detailed and broad perspective on Diné masculinities. I found the men's perspectives to be in correlation with a historical Diné matrix. In a Diné matrix, the iiná living stage is roughly between the ages of thirty and seventy-five. Most of the thirty men are over the age of thirty and are living meaningful and prosperous lives. The younger men in the study are starting to work on the life goals they want to accomplish. They also have a fresh perspective on Diné masculinities. I include elderly men, who are reflecting on their life experiences. They have lived longer lives and have experienced more. They are beginning to share what they have learned in their lifetimes. Each man provides valuable knowledge and thought to the question of what it means to be a Diné man.

In the 2010 US Census, 332,129 individuals identified as Navajo.[1] Of those individuals, 173,667 live on the Navajo reservation and off-reservation trust land.[2] In the 2000 US Census the number of Navajo men who graduated from college living on the Navajo Nation was over 4,300 in comparison with over 6,800 women.[3] In the 2010 American Community Survey, over 13,500 men and women were estimated to have an associate degree or higher living on the Navajo reservation and off-reservation trust land.[4] Twelve of the men are college graduates, seven are professionals, and the rest graduated from high school but did not attend college. Seven of the men live on the Navajo reservation, and the rest live in towns and cities in Arizona and New Mexico. The majority of the thirty men are bilingual, speaking Diné and English fluently; a few only speak English. Five of the men are military veterans. Fourteen are single and have never been married. A majority of the men play sports, are married, and have children. Four are divorced. Six men are less than thirty years old.

Only three of the interviews were digitally recorded. The rest did not want to be recorded. Instead, I wrote notes, which I verified with them later for clarity and certainty. All of the interviews lasted an hour or longer. I conducted follow-up interviews with all of the men to discuss their thoughts on relationships between Diné men and women. All of the men cooperated, and I respected what they did and did not want to include. All of the names of the men are pseudonyms to ensure their protection. Any errors or misinterpretation falls on the author and not on the men.

The methodology to acquire the information is an interdisciplinary approach combining Linda Tuhiwai Smith's indigenous project of storytelling and gendering with the Western inquiry strategy of narrative research. The approach is a distinct method to discuss, interpret, and analyze present-day Diné masculinities. This methodology ensures that the views and feelings of Diné masculinities are respected and not dismissed. I did not want the methodology and research experience to be similar to other research projects on indigenous peoples where knowledge is not reported back and shared. As Smith states:

> It appalls us that the West can desire, extract, and claim ownership of our ways of knowing, our imagery, the things we create and produce, and then simultaneously reject the people who created and developed those ideas and seek to deny them further opportunities to be creators of their own culture and own nations.[5]

This research project contributes a perspective on what it means to be an indigenous man and, more specifically, a hastiin. It is hoped that future studies on indigenous masculinities will continue and similar methods will be chosen.

The following sections highlight my discussions with the thirty men on male development, performance, and the impact of colonization on their masculinities.

Male Development

It must be stated in preface that the men's perspectives cannot be arbitrarily applied to all Diné men, though similar views might come from other men answering the same questions. This similarity should not stereotype Diné men. Diné communities have always been diverse, and individual Diné will differ in opinion.

The first question was, how did the man's parents/guardians raise him? Several of the participants stressed that their parents raised them with both Diné and American values. Steve Allison, thirty-two years old, sums up his upbringing with, "My parents stressed the Navajo language and American education. At home, my parents spoke to me in Navajo. They taught me Navajo values. They encouraged me to do well in school, and later they supported me attending college."[6] Peter Walker, twenty-seven years old, stresses his Diné upbringing:

> My mother is a "traditional" Diné, and my father does not follow any religion in particular, and for a lot of years we just called him an atheist. But he admitted he has his own unique spirituality. My mother always took us kids, my sister and two brothers, to her family's reservation homes during breaks from school in Albuquerque, so we grew up with mainly traditional Diné spiritual beliefs and influences that our family (our mother and us kids) have adopted.[7]

Several other men have similar responses. John Brown, a thirty-four year old, says, "Ever since I can remember, my parents have always been there for me physically, spiritually, and emotionally."[8] Ron Palmer, thirty-two years old, says his whole family raised him. Phillip Lester, fifty-nine years old, had a similar upbringing to Palmer's: "I was treated with care and love, though not verbally expressed."[9]

Several individuals differ in their upbringings. Paul Yazzie, sixty-eight years old, grew up quickly. He is the oldest of his siblings, and he took care of his brothers and sisters because his father was not there for the family. He says, "I was first in the family, and I had more responsibilities. I was expected to take care of my younger siblings. I learned to be reliable, and that helped me take care of my own children later on."[10] Yazzie is an exception among the men, because he became a father figure to the rest of his brothers and sisters early in his life.

Albert Burns's grandmother raised him. He was always with her herding sheep. Albert Burns is fifty-plus years old.

Barry Ryan, twenty-three years old, lived close to his paternal grandparents. They introduced him to, and influenced, his learning where he became exposed to ceremonial knowledge and worked in the cornfields. Ryan learned some cultural teachings based on the concept of what not to do in life.

Eric Gorman, forty-four years old, grew up without his parents. His grandmother on his father's side raised him. However, his grandmother did not teach him cultural knowledge. According to Gorman, he grew up experiencing tremendous hardship without any family support.

Troy Mann, thirty-three years old, also grew up without family support. He says, "My parents never really taught me what to do and what not to do, how to act, how to conduct myself, how to have a relationship, and having a family should be."[11] While the majority of the men grew up with strong family influences, other individuals grew up primarily on their own with very little family support.

The second question focused on whether or not the men grew up by the Diné development model discussed by Martin D. Topper and G. Mark Schoepfle in "Becoming a Medicine Man: A Means to Successful Midlife Transition among Traditional Navajo Men." Several individuals knew aspects of this male development model. Matthew Billison, fifty-one years old, learned extensively about his great-grandfather's life. He says, "My father's father was a medicine man. He provided examples of what lies ahead in life and what you need to do. I ran, snow bathed, and got up early."[12] While Billison learned some cultural teachings, Frank Begay, a forty-year-old, learned other Diné cultural aspects. Begay learned to take care of the livestock and home.

> They taught me a lot, the role as being a young man and then later on the role of being a man in Navajo society. It began with herding sheep. I started at five years old. As I got older, I chopped wood, hauled water, took care of the corral. I took care of things around the home. I have always been told the physical aspects of housekeeping belong to men, outside of the home. My parents and relatives influence me.[13]

Begay believes taking care of, and being responsible for, duties around the home is a lesson needed for young boys to mature into men.

Tom Cooper, forty-five years old, also learned aspects of the Diné life stage model. His grandfather was a medicine man who modeled what it meant to be a hastiin. His grandfather taught him the do's and do not's of life, and Cooper grew up in a hogan. He claims, "I lived with my grandfather in a hogan with no electricity and running water."[14]

Michael Wagner's father helped his development: "When I turned twelve my father took over my growth and development. I was made to run early in the mornings, and he made me work outside the home."[15] Michael Wagner is fifty-eight years old. Bruce Jackson's father also taught him about the Diné life stage model, but his father never forced it on him. Bruce Jackson is twenty-eight years old.

Sherman Ross's family introduced him to the táchéii, which he continues to partake in. Sherman Ross is twenty-six years old.

All six learned some aspect of the Diné life stage model, yet all learned American attitudes, behaviors, values, and beliefs. In the twenty-first century, almost all young Diné men and women grow up with American influences. Many of them learn to speak English first; they spend most of their time interacting in the English language and away from their great-grandparents, who probably speak Diné consistently. Mostly they work, go to school, watch television, listen to music, read, and do many other things within an American framework.

The third question was, what impact did American influences—such as American popular culture, school, or Christianity—have on the upbringing of these men? Overall, many of the men say American popular culture and Christianity had no effect at all on their development as men. Mel Ernest, thirty-five years old, did not watch television while growing up. His parents and extended family were strict and did not allow it. Scott Gordon, thirty-eight years old, also did not watch very much television in his childhood. His parents and extended family told him not to watch too much television because he would lose focus in life and it would create imbalance and disrupt his well-being.

The majority of the men feel school did influence their growth as a person. Most of them feel they got the education they "needed" to make a living. Some of the men went to boarding schools, and the majority attended public schools. Gabriel Porter, forty-seven years old, spent a significant amount of his education in boarding school. He feels that influenced his development as a man. He says, "The boarding school experience was very influential in development as a Navajo man because it was void of anything Navajo. I was taught to be a white American-Anglo-Christian man. I started to live two lives: Navajo, and being a white American-Anglo-Christian. I started to compartmentalize my life as a man as being Navajo and American."[16] Bill Alexander, forty-two years old, also says his boarding school experience, particularly the dormitory workers, influenced his development. The male dormitory workers maintained strict rules on how a Diné boy should behave in different situations, from maintaining the dormitory quarters to attending classes to resolving conflicts to interacting with other students. For many Diné boys, starting in the late 1940s and continuing to this day, boarding school is a home away from home and may influence their development more so than their mothers or fathers.

While some Diné boys had a positive experience with boarding schools, others did not. Scott Gordon feels boarding schools were very damaging to many of his fellow male classmates. He says, "Several were sexually, emotionally, and mentally abused by staff or even students. To this day, this cycle of abuse has never been revealed to outside sources. Many of these male students who are now grown have many relationship problems in their own lives. They cannot trust anyone, and most are alone."[17] Adam Blake, forty-one years old, attended Sherman Indian School in Riverside, California, but he never saw any abuses.

While quite a few of the men learned some Diné cultural knowledge, several did not and grew up only with American teachings. Moreover, Christianity influenced a few of the men in their childhoods, but most do not attend Christian churches or services, or practice Christianity.

Walter Johnson, thirty-seven years old, is an exception. He is influenced by the dominant culture's ways; even then he learned a few cultural aspects such as attending healing ceremonies or participating in Native American Church (NAC) ceremonies. School influenced how he views masculinity. He recognizes the negative characteristics of being a man based on what he learned from his family. He explains, "I observed how other guys behaved and what was macho. I didn't get into things that were too macho, because it went against what I already perceived from my uncle or father as being wrong or too extreme. Young men at school would address a woman as ma'am."[18] Johnson and all the Diné men interviewed regarded school as the opportunity to learn the skills and knowledge they needed as adults. Sports in school helped the men to develop their physical strength and coordination. Allison affirms this when he says, "Sports in high school developed strength and coordination which is needed to do manly activities such as cleaning the yard outside."[19] School plays a key and significant role in the development of these men.

Family also significantly influences growth. The degree of impact varies for each man, but Peter Walker's response to the question of family influence sums up, for many men interviewed, the importance of family in their childhood.

> I saw this inner strength in my uncles. The uncle I was closest to was sensitive at times. Even though I was just a kid, he would talk to me on road trips about his strained relationship with his wife and always was kind to my mother, aunts, and grandmother in a providing way, but I also seen him carry bales of hay in a blizzard on a muddy, barely passable reservation road at night with his bare hands red from the cold bailing wire. He seemed to have this raw survival instinct, an almost fearless strength to him, yet was quiet, friendly, and lived according to Diné traditions. He wasn't perfect, and sometimes drank heavily as a young man, but his inner strength and desire to help his own family and his kids is something I will never forget about him. He showed me how to live as a Diné man.[20]

Walker learned attributes of Diné men from his closest uncle. Each man's father, or a male relative, influenced his development. Adam Blake was influenced heavily by his extended family. In fact, he sought out relatives to help him go on a different life path. Family influence is not consigned to adolescent years or early twenties. Family plays a strong role in male development at any point in a man's life. Blake is an example of one whose extended family influenced his development as a man later in his life. While more Diné families are probably not teaching cultural ways, people are learning, including this group of men, traits of a Diné matrix and a way of life from a variety of sources. Their fathers, mothers, aunts, uncles, grandparents, and relatives had a strong influence on how these thirty men developed.

What Diné traits did these men learn from their families, peers, and friends? Matthew Billison learned to get up early in the morning, run, and bathe in the snow. Others learned to herd sheep, take care of the livestock, and care for the family. Hank Masters, thirty-six years old, learned to start the day appropriately. He says, "Start every day by meeting the day, for example, it's the time you make your prayers."[21] All the men learned some cultural quality, but each has been impacted by an American education. They developed their skills and knowledge in schools, yet retained the qualities they acquired from their family in childhood. Ernest learned to have self-respect and understood the do's and do not's in life.

Ryan distinguishes his Diné masculinity based on his appearance. He wears his long hair in a tsiiyéél (hair bun), has two earrings, and wears turquoise jewelry. He does not dress this way to stand out among other Diné men, but so the Diyin Dine'é can recognize him as a Diné man. Diné people wear turquoise jewelry and put their hair in a tsiiyéél, so the Diyin Dine'é can recognize them as Diné to protect the individual and community. Henry Etsitty, twenty-five years old, learned to work hard and be helpful. Etsitty observed his father working long, hard hours. He models his attitude and behavior on the idea of working ethically for others.

Several of the men also mentioned an intertribal influence in their male development. Kurt Jason, twenty-three years old, feels acquiring knowledge from intertribal organizations such as the National Congress of American Indians and the National Indian Gaming Association helps to develop character. For many young Diné and other indigenous men, working with other indigenous peoples is common. These interactions do influence how Diné peoples view indigenous peoples in general, and the world. David Francis, fifty-one years old, is involved with the Phoenix area Indian community and he interacts with many indigenous peoples from all over the United States in such ways that he has learned much from them. Gary Jones, forty years old, says powwows offered him the opportunity to observe other Native men and their responsibilities to their families and Native Nations. Furthermore, he observed other indigenous ceremonies and activities. While interacting with other indigenous peoples is mostly positive, a couple of the men mentioned a negative impact. Blake sees powwows and NAC as creating a patriarchal and Plains Indian male image and not Diné at all, but encompassing all indigenous peoples to be more generic.

Both American and Diné cultures have influenced the thirty Diné men. Does this mean their development is similar to all men in the United States? It is a good possibility, but not absolutely. All of these men learned certain ideas on becoming a man from American schools; however, they also learned specific Diné attributes from their families and way of life. This particular rearing must be taken into account in discussing Diné male development. Diné men have learned to be men from their families, schools, and a Diné matrix. What does this mean for the manifestation of Diné masculinities?

Male Performance

How do Diné men express their masculinity? Does fatherhood establish their masculinity? Does participation in athletics and/or the military characterize Diné masculinity? Do violence and/or love establish Diné masculinity? Does the Diné language define your manhood? Does participation in healing ceremonies and rituals denote Diné masculinity? What is the role of a hastiin? These questions direct this section.

The first question is, how do they express their Diné masculinities? Several men were taken aback by the question. For these men, they had to think about the question for a short while. They did not know exactly how to answer and/or how they confirm their masculinity. Even after thinking for a short while, some still did not know exactly how to answer the question. In fact, David Francis responds with, "Ummm…in the past I guess for me it was how many girlfriends. Now I don't know."[22] Francis's answer is not typical of the other men. Brian Erickson, a forty-eight-year-old, answers the question more comprehensively: "Accepting traditions, talking the Navajo language fully, understanding the culture, having knowledge about the government and history, but also taking care and providing food, clothing, and other items for your family."[23] Erickson and Francis represent the extremes of the responses. Tom Cooper, Frank Begay, Matthew Billison, and Gabriel Porter all had similar views on this question. Their answers focus on taking responsibility and providing for the family. Cooper's answer was the most basic when he stated plainly, "What I do."[24] Frank Begay had a more elaborate answer. He expresses, "Taking responsibility for your actions and decisions and providing for the family. It also has to do with understanding your emotional side of things."[25] Gary Jones focuses his answer on the cultural teachings: "By taking part in winter dances and helping out with the family stuff or ceremonies."[26] Bill Alexander also focuses on cultural teachings when answering the question. He accepts his role, along with the obligations and duties, as an uncle. He expects to interact with family members and other people, demonstrate and instill discipline within the family, be a spokesperson for the family, and to be a provider for the family. Henry Etsitty expresses his masculinity by working hard, not complaining, and being helpful to others. Peter Walker expands on Cooper, Begay, Porter, and Billison's response of provider:

> I try to improve on my life every day. I wake up and strive to get something accomplished every day whether it be for me, my family, or outside community. I also try to research, study, and learn about Diné history and worldviews. I try to follow what customs and spirituality I was taught. I'm not perfect and have not always lived my life like this, but maturing is a part of becoming a man and aging. I also wear something turquoise almost every day. One reason I wear turquoise is because it clarifies for other people whether I am Native American or not. I also wear it because I see Diné men in old black and white photographs wearing it, but I also wear it to be recognized as a Diné by the holy ones.[27]

Basically, the men express their masculinity in the actions they take, taking responsibilities for those actions, and providing for their family or love ones. For these men, masculinity is defined by their behavior and their execution of activities. Their responses appear to correlate to Michael Kimmel's self-made man, but it appears status, wealth, and social mobility are not necessarily on the minds of these men.[28] This does not mean they do not want to acquire wealth and status; perhaps they have reached a point in their lives where taking responsibility for their actions and ensuring their family or loved ones are being taken care of is a priority.

The second question focuses on whether or not fatherhood establishes Diné masculinities. The majority of the men are fathers. Eight of the men do not have children. The majority of the men stated fatherhood does establish Diné masculinity while four said it did not. Two others said maybe. The men who answered yes believe fatherhood does confirm Diné masculinity, because men can develop their minds, teach the knowledge they know, model maturity, and create opportunities for their children to be responsible and to care for their families. Billison responds with, "Yes. A father can be firm and discipline his children and then be gentle and explain the issues and stuff."[29]

Fatherhood shows and imparts Diné masculinity to the children and to the extended family. The men who replied no did not believe creating an offspring automatically proves you are a man. More so, these men felt taking care of and raising your children helps verify masculinity. Walker expresses, "No, simply creating offspring does not establish manhood. It proves your manhood if you are a father to your children. I think putting forth effort in raising your kids in a positive way proves your manhood."[30] Answering no does not mean fatherhood has no place in affirming Diné masculinity, but rather that the actions of the man to serve and take care of the children equates to being a hastiin.

The two who responded with maybe had entirely different reasons for their views. The first man focused on the opportunity for the individual to support his children with a sense of hope, admiration, and the motivation for the family to succeed. The individual has a chance to be a provider and create stability in the family and to sustain hope. The second person focused extensively on sexual relations. He states, "I think fatherhood partially establishes your manhood because fatherhood means you had sex with a woman. And an adult male proves his manhood by sexual activity with a woman. This shows his role as a male."[31] He thinks the physical act of having sex with a woman helps establish a man's masculinity. This viewpoint is similar to the studies done by Kimmel and other scholars researching American masculinities. Does having sex with a woman establish a Diné man's masculinity? To one Diné man, the answer is yes. For others, it was not part of the discussion.

The third question is whether or not military and/or athletic participation characterizes Diné masculinities. For American society, the answer is absolutely as Burstyn, Wakefield, hooks, and others illustrate. Diné communities since the early twentieth century have sent men to Europe, Asia, Africa, and other parts of the world to fight for the United States in many conflicts. During World War II, hundreds of Diné men trained as code talkers, and they fought in the Pacific Theater against the Japanese. Hundreds of Diné families have sons, fathers, and uncles serving in the military today. Among the interviewed men, there was no consensus on military participation confirming Diné masculinities. Cooper feels military participation gives Diné men something to do—a job. Erickson thinks the military develops a man's mind, creates discipline, and encourages the man to be appropriate. Billison equates today's military to past Diné protectors. He describes this similarity: "Participation in the military is like being a warrior. Navajo men are raised to be a warrior, to take on life's challenges. The military prepares these men for life."[32] Porter sees military and athletic participation as a way for a man to find acceptance among other men. Other men do not share Billison's view. Yazzie adamantly states, "No. That is a false image of a better man. A man is to talk and act in a gentle way. He is to respect the elderly and help people."[33] Wagner concurs with Yazzie: "Unfortunately, for many Diné men, athletics and/or military training do define manhood. The problem here is both athletics and the military are not truly organic or indigenous to Diné male identity. Instead, they are 'add ons' and assimilative in the sense that they represent Western ideals that are too problematic."[34] Begay expands on Yazzie and Wagner's comments:

> You don't need to play sports to prove yourself. You don't need to go into the military to prove you're brave. The things we face every day, you are a warrior. You have to protect what's yours, you have to protect your family, and in that sense that warrior part of you is alive and well with you every day. You don't need to go into the military to depict yourself as a warrior, but because we have always been warriors in our culture a lot of people think in that term. They say, okay, it's my duty as a Diné person to become a warrior. I am joining the military. It's my duty because it's in our bloodline. I don't really agree with that. I think military is really an option for people unless of course there's the draft. Other than that, being a warrior is facing adversity every day.[35]

Begay feels Diné peoples misinterpret what it means to be a protector. Of the men I spoke with, only five—Albert Burns, Bruce Jackson, Walter Johnson, Randy Thompson (seventy-plus years old) and Steve Allison—are veterans. All of them think military participation helps establish Diné masculinity to a certain degree. Johnson thinks the military is a bit extreme, although he recognizes military service portrays a sense of being a protector, and as a man he knows it is his duty to defend his country and family from harm. Allison also reiterates the idea of a man's role to protect. Jackson spent four years in the United States Navy, but it does not define him as a hastiin. Burns feels the military and athletics help men to stay physically and mentally fit only. Thompson served three years in the armed services where his masculinity was further redefined. He feels the military helped him understand more about himself and his masculinity.

When it comes to athletics, the answers are similar. Half of the men feel sports does not denote Diné masculinities while the other half feel it does. Almost all the men played basketball, football, baseball, or some sort of outdoor sport. Allison feels athletics helps a man develop a physical body and good coordination. Gorman agrees with Allison, as his children are participating in sports now. Walker replies, "I like lifting weights to make myself look masculine, and it helps me feel like a man, knowing I could go outside and I am strong enough to work at whatever, but it doesn't define my manhood."[36] Porter thinks athletic participation is a good outlet for male "wildness." Some Diné men appear to follow American male views on athletics and the military, such as that military participation fulfills the historical role of being a protector while athletics helps build the physical body. However, those views are not unified.

The fourth and fifth questions focus on violence and love. With the exception of three individuals, the men say violence does not establish Diné masculinity. Gorman thinks violence probably establishes Diné masculinity as he recalled his extended family getting into fights and family relatives being angry at each other. Alcohol was often present in those situations, which inevitably led to violence. Burns also thinks violence does establish Diné masculinities, but not in a respectful way. Allison is one of the men who did not say no, but his response is on the ability to protect people from violence. He declares:

> I think the ability to address violence does. In a unit of a man and woman, the man's role is to defend and protect that unit. In that role of defense and protection, the man needs to be able to defend against hostility that is all around us in our environment. This hostility can be physical, mental, social, political, and even spiritual.[37]

While violence is viewed as negative, protection is the opposite of it. Allison believes neither can exist without the other. In Diné thought, all things in life encompass positive and negative energies. At times, one will be stronger than the other.

When I posed the question on love, the majority of the men expressed that love does establish Diné masculinities. They stated love is not exclusive to a spouse or girlfriend but includes family, children, and all living things. The men think love and compassion helps them to be in touch with their spirituality, and displays the notion that men can take risks and be responsible for their actions. Only three men thought love did not establish Diné masculinities. They did not elaborate on this statement. They merely thought love did not equate to masculinity. Their views are similar to the myth that men do not espouse/declare love. Women openly declare love, not men, but the majority of the Diné men in this study do not see it this way. They see love and the declaration of it as being human. When you examine SNBH, you understand where some of the men are coming from in regards to love establishing Diné masculinities. SNBH is a reflection of male and female essences, and love is equated to humanity, therefore love is not separate for each gender, but rather love is part of each gender. Love is embedded in humanity, life, and the cosmos.

The next question focused on the Diné language. Half of the men felt speaking the Diné language did not confirm Diné masculinities. All of these men are educated in American schools, and all speak English. The English language directs their mindsets. Some of the men do not speak Diné, so one element of a distinct Diné matrix is lacking. They can only express themselves in the English language. Some men do know how to speak Diné, but they feel Diné men who do not speak the language fluently are not less Diné and are not less men. However, they felt the language expresses what it "truly" means to be a hastiin. The men, however, are in a dilemma regarding language and its connection to Diné masculinities. Frank Begay states, "That's really hard to say because the majority of our people are losing that portion of it. It's really hard to say. I can say it does, or I can say it does not. I guess a lot of the questions depend on where you are at, on the reservation or off."[38] John Brown did not think speaking Diné defined his masculinity, but he acknowledged the importance of the language to Diné identity: "No. However, the Navajo language is important to the future of Diné society and it is important to understanding your role as a Diné man."[39] Phillip Lester took an open approach to his answer: "Any language would, when spoken in positive tones."[40] Speaking the Diné language and not speaking the Diné language does define Diné masculinities among the thirty men.

Participating in healing ceremonies affirms Diné masculinities for all the men except three. Diné men learn the ideals of masculinities from their puberty ceremony and sweats. Allison confirms, "There are certain rules for men and women in ceremonial rituals. For example, in the large ceremonies, men sit on one side of the hogan while women sit in another part. This puts people in one group or another. Certain ceremonies are also directly addressing the topic of manhood such as puberty ceremonies for males."[41] The male puberty ceremony teaches boys the stories, values, and skills needed as a hastiin. Johnson affirms this role:

> Yes, I gather ideals associated with maleness, and try to portray them in real life, i.e., Monster Slayer being the defender of the people from monsters. Songs about him are spiritually blessed upon you, and you get this sense of a warrior and feel protected.[42]

Learning the stories, songs, and prayers from ceremonies scaffolds Diné male identity. Learning to protect their families, teaching the cultural ways, and loving all things are foundational traits in a Diné man's life. Most of the men in this study believe ceremonial participation authenticates Diné male identity, however three disagree. Bruce Jackson says, "It used to, prior to my conversion to biblical Christianity, but now it no longer does."[43] Troy Mann concurs: "I don't believe so. To me, it is more of a belief for the Navajo people, tradition."[44] They believe Diné masculinity is what the man makes of his life. For these individuals, masculinity is structured on what he does and the responsibility of his behavior. Their viewpoints are not much different from the rest of the men, except that Diné ceremonial participation does not sanction masculinities.

The last question focused on a Diné man's function in life. In the past, men protected and provided for the extended family and clan community. For several of the men, they reiterate this notion. Allison simply states, "The same— protection, strength-activities, and bringing home food."[45] Randy Thompson agrees with Allison. Thompson states the role of a Diné man in the twenty-first century is the same as yesterday. Others expand on these statements such as

Erickson, who details the male role: "Educator, bringing up a family, teaching the language and culture to the family and the people, and to be a leader among the people."[46] Ron Palmer agrees with Erickson: "To support your family and friends. To protect and stand up for what you believe."[47] Albert Burns extends Erickson and Palmer's answers when he says, "Being a mentor to their relatives and younger people."[48] Gabriel Porter and Sherman Ross feel cultural teachings are part of a man's role. Porter believes Diné men need to perpetuate their ancestor's values. Ross believes men need to share cultural teachings within the family and to teach children how to be independent.

Several of the men also spoke about being a leader for the people. Leadership qualities are taught to young boys early in their lives and strengthened during the puberty ceremonies. Leadership encompasses more than acquiring or possessing authority and power. Leadership in Diné communities employs the ability to eloquently speak for the people and intelligently find solutions to the problems at hand. Power and authority has nothing to do with Diné leadership. However, it appears some Diné men in tribal government have forgotten this understanding. Some of the men commented about being a leader, yet only one illustrated the specifics on how to do this in the twenty-first century. Michael Wagner says, "It would be to assist Diné society in reconstruction of culture, language, and interdependent socialization processes, given that we must also live in the modern world. It is to help produce critical thinkers, nurturing, and engaged Diné citizens and community members."[49]

Johnson and Walker refine the role of a provider and protector. Walker states:

> I think helping our Diné people out in our own way, by whatever means. Whether that be working to correct our mistakes, taking care of our children in a decent way, working for the tribe, or practicing our culture, we should be mindful on improving the lives of our people in some form of fashion through whatever contribution. I want to look back on my life knowing I contributed to the overall welfare of the Diné in some way.[50]

Johnson takes a similar approach, but he believes life is vastly different than three hundred years ago. He incorporates American ways of thinking and living with Diné thought. He says, "To adapt to changes and to live in a multicultural society. I think he has to manipulate current cultural norms to fit in with the times. He has to be more focus than ever, because there are more distractions than before."[51] Kurt Jason contrasts Diné men living on the reservation with those living in urban cities. He believes Diné men who live on the reservation want to leave and earn an education. This education can be helpful for the Navajo Nation. Urban Diné men on the other hand might take a different approach, but Jason does not elaborate.

Barry Ryan believes Diné male roles are to be balanced with female roles in the communities. He believes Diné women are self-reliant and do not necessarily have to rely on men to be the provider and protector, but that Diné men have certain responsibilities for the family, clan, and community. Diné men must not do anything to harm the family or bring shame. According to Ryan, a Diné man's goal is to better the family and to bring prosperity.

Scott Gordon emphasizes the need for a positive role model for the family, clan, and Diné peoples. According to Gordon, a role model creates self-respect, develops purpose in life, and enhances a man's identity. Henry Etsitty believes the role for Diné men is to live for the next generations. Diné men are to help Diné women live a peaceful and good life. They are to protect their families from the "monsters of this world." They are to destroy the bad things in life.

The role and responsibility of a Diné man is to work for the continuation of a Diné way of life. They are to provide and protect for their extended families, clan communities, and to strive for happiness and prosperity. They are to use the tools and knowledge of the world to make it happen. The men believe they are adhering to the twin protectors in their own personal lives.

Today, Diné men validate their masculinities by what they do on a daily basis. While some men think military and athletic participation shows they are indeed men, historical Diné male attributes continue. The first priority of a man is to be a complementary partner to a woman. The men believe a man must take responsibility for his own actions, and he must show compassion and love. Half of the men think fatherhood does inform Diné masculinities, and if the man becomes a father he must be responsible to his wife and children. The act of violence does not establish Diné masculinities, but the ability to combat it in confrontations is an attribute. Speaking the Diné language does not necessarily contribute to Diné masculinities, however the Diné language is important to the future of the Navajo Nation and to understanding a person's role and responsibility on the Earth and in the universe. Ceremonial participation does establish Diné masculinities, and a man must partake in the puberty ceremony to begin his journey as a hastiin. Overall, the responses from the men demonstrate how they incorporate historical Diné masculinity traits with contemporary ways of thinking and living. This creates a distinct perspective on Diné masculinities, and the history of colonization can help explain why.

Colonization/Transformation

Has living in America changed Diné masculinities? Has Christianity transformed Diné masculinities? Has speaking English altered Diné masculinities? Does participation in the Native American Church influence Diné masculinities? Most of the men state Diné masculinities have been transformed, but to what degree, they do not know. The extent of these changes and how this impacts a Diné way of life is where discussion needs to take place.

Diné communities have incorporated American attitudes, values, and beliefs. Diné history shows the peoples incorporating different tools, and knowledge, and molding them to fit their families and clans. Diné peoples in the twenty-first century are doing the same, however many have either never learned or forgotten the stories, songs, prayers, and cultural knowledge their ancestors acquired through experience and observation.

Some Diné speak English primarily and have no knowledge or competence of the cultural teachings. They live differently than their ancestors from two hundred-plus years ago. Yet, not all of the men think Diné masculinities have changed significantly. Yazzie feels basically no detrimental change has occurred, because Diné peoples continue to speak the language, perform the healing ceremonies, herd sheep, grow corn, and think in Diné. He also feels speaking English has not change Diné men directly. In fact, English has enhanced Diné communities. Begay concurs: "Speaking English and Navajo has made us powerful."[52] Ken Lee, fifty-seven years old, also feels Diné masculinities are influenced by speaking English and practicing Christianity, but those markers do not change the fundamental meaning of Diné masculinities for him.

Most of the men express that the dominant American lifestyle has altered Diné masculinities. Walker explains his reasoning:

The history between the US and the Diné is not good most of the time. I think our people are still recovering from this horrible history. I think it can be difficult sometimes as a Diné man to keep our heads up in the face of the outside world and all the internal problems the Diné nation faces. I think it may be easy to escape from it all through alcohol or drugs, or adopting the ways of non-Natives to gain material wealth or prosperity. We have to adopt some of those ways, but we also can't forget who we are or where we come from. Diné men today are different from our ancestors in terms of education, English language usage, and the pursuit of different careers. We today are different than the men that were born fifty years ago, with the nature of rapidly advancing technology and also in numbers of population and opportunities. I'm sure fifty years from now the life of the Diné man will also be very different.[53]

If American standards of living and values have transformed Diné masculinities, does practicing and believing in Christianity have the same impact on the men? Most of the men think so. Cooper replies, "Quite a bit. Navajo way of thinking and believing is all in English today. Not all of it is bad though."[54] John Brown agrees with most of the men, but he feels practicing Christianity is a choice. He says, "I think that Christianity can be left out of your life if you want to, unlike capitalism. That is, you can practice your traditional practices without ever being concerned by the influence of Christianity."[55] Several of the men feel Christianity influences Diné men who are having an identity crisis. Allison believes this quagmire creates men who develop into alcoholics or feel a state of worthlessness. He says:

I think Christianity was the force imposed upon Native Americans because Native Americans were considered heathens (non-Christians). This permitted the early English-Americans to slaughter Native Americans relentlessly. Today, Native American men of various tribes have poor self-esteem because they feel like they are subdued. Therefore, many of the Navajo men, no longer warrior-like, and feeling worthless, drink and become alcoholics.[56]

Hank Masters feels Christianity makes some Diné men critical of other men for their lack of faith, but he feels Christianity makes these men less than their counterparts. He describes the situation thus:

> Yes, when other Navajo males (not just adult males) come to me with Christian, Mormon, or whatever beliefs that they have taken on, and look down their nose at you if you don't agree with them. They judge you. How stupid, or is it ignorant, can you get? When they look at themselves in the mirror they are no longer looking at themselves through their own eyes. They are ashamed, thus they are beaten.[57]

Both Masters and Allison feel Christianity has a deep impact on Diné men. Walker concurs:

> I think the pressure of Christian conversion and also boarding schools has affected some Diné men in profound ways. If they were not trying to kill us, they were trying to convert us. It is not as clear-cut as that, but it is almost. My cousin lived with a Mormon family as a teen, was converted, and became a devout follower. Then after his mission he came home and eventually started drinking, dropped out of college, and now lives at home, and now nearly forty years old is employed at a fast food restaurant in the Gallup area. He doesn't know the language or culture and I think for a lot of years he was confused and torn between the ways of his people and homeland and that of the Mormons.[58]

Kurt Jason has uncles on his father side who are pastors of Christian churches. His uncles teach how to live life according to the gospel. Jason follows the Christian Reform religion and believes Christianity has changed how Diné men think, act, and behave positively.

Not all of the men feel Christianity has changed Diné masculinities. Burns does not think so. He feels Diné Christians stay to their religious roles and stories and do not venture into Diné beliefs and stories. Begay thinks Christianity can change Diné men because the concept of man controlling all things is espoused in the Christian faith and is not part of Diné spirituality, although he is somewhat uncertain. Erickson discusses how Diné men need to balance both Diné and Christian values and beliefs. Jackson takes Erickson's thoughts further: "Biblical Christianity has changed only those Navajo men who put their trust in God. But as far as those who don't believe, Biblical Christianity has not changed them, or their manhood."[59] Most Diné men in this study do not believe Christianity has radically altered Diné masculinities, but it appears Christianization impacts how Diné masculinities are viewed by Diné peoples.

The Native American Church formed in the late nineteenth and early twentieth centuries, where NAC combined Christianity with the taking of peyote, a cactus viewed as a sacrament. The United States formally recognized NAC in the early twentieth century. NAC is practiced throughout the Western hemisphere including the Navajo reservation. Many indigenous peoples in the United States are NAC participants.

Walter Johnson says NAC gives a deeper understanding of a Diné way of life and helps men maintain a spiritual guardianship. He says NAC meetings include Diné cultural knowledge. Henry Etsitty has also recently been influenced by NAC. His father credits NAC in helping him to stop drinking alcohol. Etsitty credits both NAC and Diné spirituality with helping him to understand his place as a man. Gary Jones also credits NAC. He says:

> I think the Native American Church did benefit me as a Navajo man. I had the opportunity to experience the connection of being a Native American and being Navajo. Even the ceremony was conducted in the tepee and the conduct was something I had not experience before, I had the opportunity to question who I was as a Native American. It showed me the responsibility of being a Native man, and before I did not have that type of connection to being a young man. I think it was an eye opener to be given the opportunity to see that I had a responsibility of being native and being Navajo with a purpose to provide, protect, learn, and become a man.[60]

Both of these men believe NAC has some influence in Diné male development, but to what degree is the question. Etsitty says young men are interested in Diné spirituality, but he sees more of them learning to sing NAC songs and not the beauty way songs. He feels NAC songs are easier to learn, and ceremonies are easier to remember. Jones thinks NAC does have a part in influencing Diné male development. Adam Blake also thinks NAC has an impact, but he feels it reconnects men to spirituality and brotherhood rather than Diné revitalization. Bruce Jackson says young men around the reservation think eagle fans, a robe, and a teepee signify Diné culture and tradition.

Steve Allison believes NAC has had a definite impact on Diné peoples, positive and negative. He states:

> Once the Navajo wars have ended with the long walk, incarceration, and the treaty restraints, Navajo men discontinued the Navajo warrior tradition that was based upon the Navajo traditional culture. Without the wars, Navajo men have lost their pride and have become disillusioned. As a result, they turned to alcohol or joined the American military or both. When peyote was introduced, a lot of Navajo men turned to peyote to escape the wrath of alcoholism. As to masculinity, the peyote religion discourages alcohol abuse and teaches how to be a good, responsible, and proper person. A lot of people see these teachings in the peyote religion as good. I think this is the reason about a third of Navajos today follow the peyote religion. On the other hand, roadmen are also accused of committing adultery with their patients and patient's wives through ceremonial power. So it goes both ways. Peyote can be helpful as well as hurtful to masculinity.[61]

Other Diné men have no connection to NAC. For some, like Gabriel Porter and Peter Walker, it is a foreign religion similar to Christianity. Overall, the majority of the thirty men believe NAC has no impact on Diné masculinities, however for many Diné men and women, who are NAC members, it does have a significant influence.

The next question is whether or not being individualistic and focusing their energy on only their immediate family has changed Diné masculinities.

The responses are equally yes and no. The men who say yes believe men only think of themselves and their immediate family and not their extended and clan families anymore. Allison declares, "Yes, our ideas of the protecting role of men have changed. The degree of protection seems to have changed. Rather than protecting the extended family, today men think for themselves and/or protecting only their immediate families."[62] Erickson concurs with Allison's viewpoint, but he points out that in the United States married men focus on their immediate family needs and wants. Diné men are merely following what they have learned from American society. Mel Ernest catches himself telling his family certain items are only for immediate family usage not for others. He realizes in the past, people in the community always would share what they had, but now it has changed. People seem to be concerned for their own well-being, not for other peoples in the community.

The men who disagreed believe other factors have more impact, such as school, work, and relocation. Billison believes Diné communities have always been individualistic, because he learned to be self-sufficient and independent and not to rely on others. He learned Diné peoples have always been self-reliant as demonstrated by taking care of the sheep and grazing the land. He does not think Diné peoples learn to be individualistic from Americans. Porter agrees with Billison. He says, "Navajos have always had individualism. My wife is Jemez and they are more communal than Navajo."[63] Begay feels, in some cases, Diné men practice individualism in situations when they abuse their family and/or wife. Another is when they choose not to help the extended family with a legitimate request. Alexander feels individualism and attentiveness to the immediate family is no different than in the past. He believes men who are individualistic are more resourceful and more responsible for the family. He also believes individualism and attentiveness to the immediate family helps men and women survive in this world.

Diné peoples always encouraged and promoted individuality in their families and communities. They did not stress the notion of individualism, or an individual's pursuits rather than a collective's needs. The extended families and clans' interests were paramount to individual needs and wants. If individuals pursued their own wants, they were banished from the community. While self-sufficiency was encouraged, there were limitations to try to prevent individuals from pursuing their own selfish wants.

The final question focused on the impact all non-Diné entities and institutions have on a collective Diné identity. For most of the thirty men, non-Diné entities and institutions such as the federal government, the entertainment industry, and the general American public do influence the meaning of Diné identity and masculinities. Kurt Jason believes many young Diné men develop their character based on non-Diné sources. Henry Etsitty offers his initial observations pertaining to the media:

> I do believe that Navajo perceptions of manhood have been skewed by the media images emanating from TV and movie screens. On a certain level the transformative nature of stories has changed how some Navajo men perceive themselves, thus their values. It seems that the culture of America is one that is transmitted in its art, media, press, and structure. This can be found in the way that the power structure entertains itself and the image they spin to the population about the actions they take. Subsequently the art of the people follow that tone and the TV shows, movies, books all correspond the values, needs, and wants of the power structure. From the power to the media, there is an echoing of the perpetuation that culture has created a large hegemonic group that oppresses, but insists they are the models for liberation. So yes Navajo men find this system amorous and some fully embrace their logic and they then cannot see beyond their perceptions.[64]

Scott Gordon, Gary Jones, and Gabriel Porter also have similar views as Etsitty. Gordon thinks some Diné men try to reenact barbaric behavior, drink alcohol and smoke cigarettes, be dominant over women, and abuse their own people. Porter says most Diné men and Diné peoples have no idea what it means to be Diné. He says:

> Navajo representations from non-Navajo sources such as the US government, the entertainment industry, and the world has impacted the collective identity of Navajo men and Navajo people in general. American popular culture has damaged Navajo collective identity. I still have hope in some hidden

corner of the Navajo reservation there are still real Navajos. It is disheartening to see young Navajo men trying to act like a Black rapper or Hispanic gangster. The only hope we Navajo men have for our Navajo masculinity is our Navajo women.[65]

Peter Walker says interaction with American ideas, thoughts, values, behaviors, and ways is inevitable, a must, and both positive and negative. He offers an insightful and thought-provoking perspective.

Adaptation to outside objects, tools, devices over the years such as chainsaws, trucks, and more recently computers, etc. have on the most part made positive changes for Diné men in terms of work, daily duties, employment opportunities, and work accomplishments. Yet, outside substances like alcohol, drugs, and junk food, Diné men have really struggled with over generations. Popular music and the various pop cultures associated with the different genres has been a mixed bag for Diné men over the years also. Any culture and group of people around the globe must wrestle with a decline in their languages, cultures, and traditions due to the adoption of outside influences, usually American influences, yet the pursuit of the American dream most of the time is what is most desired for a lifestyle. It is natural for people to want their youth to have better lives as a whole than they did.[66]

Walter Johnson also believes American influences are positive. He says, "As a veteran, the US government instilled discipline, self-motivation, and hard work ethics. Good people like Nelson Mandela, Ghandi, and the Dalai Lama—and how they carry themselves—influence me personally as a Navajo man to be humble."[67] However, not all agree, such is the case with Bruce Jackson. He does not think non-Diné sources impact the collective identity of Diné men and Diné peoples in general. He does see young Diné trying to attain the "good life" such as college degrees, prestige, and a professional career. Jackson feels this striving to attain the "good life" is based on individualism, self-promotion, and self-ambition. He does not believe non-Diné representations impact Diné identity.

Most of the men believe Diné masculinities have been transformed by colonization, though this belief is not universal. Speaking English, not learning and knowing the creation narratives, prayers, and songs, and not living with the land yields evidence Diné communities have been altered greatly. The degree of change leaves much for discussion, because some men think Diné masculinities and communities have changed tremendously, but how much is determined by each man and family. Diné masculinities still represent some similarities to a Diné way of life two hundred-plus years ago. America has influenced Diné men to a certain extent depending on socioeconomic and cultural conditions. Diné men blend American and Diné matrices. More young Diné men are being influenced by American way of life consequently it has altered Diné masculinities.

Conclusion

Michael Messner and Michael Kimmel have researched extensively on American masculinities. Many factors including gendered institutions and relations between different races, ethnicities, and groups have established American masculinities. Furthermore, male performance plays a role in what it means to be an American man.

According to Kimmel and others, proving one is a man has become a crisis in America.[68] Diné men in this study are similar to an extent, but significantly different than American men, although they learn American ideas about being a man.

Diné men have learned certain American attitudes on being a man such as developing your own life (Kimmel's self-made man pursuit of the late nineteenth and early twentieth centuries) and establishing your masculinity through athletics and/or military participation. Diné men are not a monolithic group, however American and Diné cultures influence Diné masculinities. Schools and families have significantly impacted how Diné men develop their masculine identity.

Diné men affirm their masculinity by what they do on a daily basis. These men intertwine American perspectives of maleness with historical Diné male attributes. They continue to provide for and protect their extended family and loved ones. They believe a man must take responsibility for his own actions, and he must show compassion and love. Fatherhood does not necessarily validate a Diné man, however if he provides for and protects his child, then he is fulfilling one of his responsibilities as a man. The ability to confront violence is another attribute of Diné men. Speaking the Diné language does not necessarily establish Diné manhood, but the thirty men believe in the continuation and importance of the language. Many of these characteristics are similar to other cultures and groups in the United States.

Participating in a male kinaaldá or other ceremonies does engender Diné masculinity even though fewer men partake in the ceremony. Most of the men in this study believe men need to balance American ideals of a man with the historical attributes of the twin protectors.

Most of the men believe colonization has changed Diné masculinities. The changes are not judged as positive or negative, but they are acknowledged and confirmed by the men. More Diné men than ever before are speaking English to the extent they do not know the creation stories, prayers, and songs of their ancestors. Despite this fact, there are still many Diné men who continue to speak their language and do know the stories, prayers, and songs. Diné communities are different, and each man represents the degree of change. These thirty men follow aspects of historical Diné masculinities even when they adopt various contemporary American perspectives on being a man.

How does this study fit into the broader discussion of American masculinities? Diné masculinities are as diverse and distinct as American masculinities. Diné communities can provide a road map on how two vastly different matrices can coexist in a distinct way where both influence how Diné men live in the twenty-first century. At times, one matrix will dominate the other and vice versa. Individual men and community influences will determine which is stronger at times. This study also illustrates a distinct male construction. Some learn aspects of the Diné male development paradigm, where hastiins mature into hastoi (elderly men). Diné masculinities are distinguishable from other cultural masculinities based on the history, their matrix, and how they work to perpetuate their way of life. The interviews do not show conformity among all Diné men, but can be a guide toward understanding Diné thought and way of life. Diné masculinities are about plurality, diversity, and openness. These values are not all different from the past, though they reflect a distinct view of life.

6
Hastiin: Twenty-First Century Diné Masculinities

Family, marriage, maturity, and a puberty ceremony help develop a Diné boy into a man. In the twenty-first century, a Diné man has a different perspective on what it means to be a hastiin. Schools and families play an enormous influence in male development and expression. Young Diné boys usually learn how to be a man through their father, mother, and/or male relative in the extended family. A man's action appears to establish his masculinity. While competing in athletics and/or joining the military has historically been a way for American men to show their masculinity, for Diné men it has not always been the case, but for some men it is moving in this direction. While many Diné men play sports and/or are in the military, they did not learn what it means to be a hastiin from those activities; his behavior, responsibilities to his family and people, and his cultural knowledge epitomize a hastiin.

Colonization, technology, and Western education have altered Diné communities. While a Diné matrix allows people to incorporate new ideas, innovations, and actions, new ways of thinking and living impact the meaning of a hastiin. The following describes these new ways of thinking and living.

The first is the adoption of the Euro-American concept of "rugged individualism" in the attitude and behavior. Diné life promotes individuality. Individuality is defined as a person's particular character, or aggregate of qualities distinguishing one person from another. A person's individuality enhanced their connection to family and community. Each person's distinct personality and character was acknowledged and appreciated. Families and communities loved each person. At times, some individuals were selfish and did not think of their responsibility to their families and communities, however by far the majority of Diné peoples understood their responsibility and obligation to their relatives and communities. They took it upon themselves to ensure the family and community continued.

Some families continue to practice communal values, although the majority of Diné peoples follow the American definition of individualism rather than the concept of Diné individuality. Diné life, two hundred-plus years ago, allowed and promoted individuality in the community. Diné men and women had roles and responsibilities to fulfill to sustain the community. Men and women hunted, planted and harvested crops, and herded sheep. These tasks allowed a person's individuality to excel, while the identity of the individual resided in the extended family and community. A Diné matrix does not promote the idea that men are superior to women or vice versa. A Diné matrix reflects the connection man has to all living things in the community whether it is the wife, the extended family, the clan family, the sense of place, or the language. Diné men in the past thought of communal priorities first, rather than their own personal wants.

In the twenty-first century, many Diné men focus on their individualism. Men work for themselves and their immediate family's needs. Many Diné women take the same approach. This affects how Diné peoples view family, individuality, and community. Anthropologist Clyde Kluckhohn observed these changes in the 1940s. He wrote:

> To live at all in this barren region the individual must have the economic cooperation of others, and such cooperation is hardly likely to come to those who deviate from the "right way of doing things" as the Navaho see it. Thus the major threat, which restrains the potential offender, is the withdrawal of the support and the good will of his neighbors, most of whom are "family" to the Navaho. Gossip and criticism were and are major means of social control throughout Navaho society. These diffuse sanctions are less effective today than in former times because, by taking up wage work for whites, the offender can escape both the need for economic cooperation by the group and the criticism which the group aims at deviators.[1]

Historically, individuality helped maintain the community. Kluckhohn described how Diné families used the social mechanisms of gossip and criticism to ensure cooperation. While gossip and criticism continue, those social tools are less effective in creating cooperation and family-centered work. Diné cooperation in the past came not from gossip and criticism but a responsibility to communal sustainability. Diné men and women worked together to ensure the community had food to eat, wood to burn to keep warm, shelter to protect them from the elements, and prosperity. The creation narratives, a person's understanding of SNBH, and the leadership organization of the community has helped individuals meet their responsibilities to the community.

Gossip and criticism creates disharmony and dislike for each other. Kluckhohn described how the notion of American individualism created disharmony and dislike:

> The introduction of the white idea of individualism without the checks and balances that accompany it leads to the failure of collective or cooperative action of every sort. The substitution of paid labor for reciprocal services is not in and of itself a bad thing. But there is not a commensurate growth of the white idea of individual responsibility. There tends to be a distortion of the whole cultural structure, which makes it difficult to preserve harmonious personal relationships and satisfying emotional adjustments. Widespread exercise of escape mechanisms, especially alcohol, is the principal symptom of the resultant friction and decay.[2]

According to Kluckhohn, Diné communities were in moral decay in the 1940s. Starting in 1946, thousands of Diné youth were sent to special vocational programs and boarding schools impacting Diné families for nine months out of the year. Their Diné values and beliefs were greatly affected. Young Diné people were indoctrinated with the attitude American ways were superior and an individual works hard to succeed even at the expense of friends, family, and others. Many Diné men changed from working for the extended family and the community's prosperity to working for the immediate family's needs and wants. In the past, Diné masculinities represented the community's prosperity rather than the individual accomplishments. It appears the reverse is happening now.

Second, Diné men work for wages. By the 1960s, many families found work in wage labor with very few negative consequences to the household. Historian Colleen O'Neill documents how men and women used wage labor to meet their household obligations. She writes:

> Resisting permanent relocation and refusing to conform to the BIA's expectations, Navajos made a place for themselves in the southwestern labor market. They participated in that market but did not embrace the assimilationist goals that BIA officials and some employers promoted. Navajos did leave the reservation to find jobs. But for many—like the Kees—that work provided them with the resources they needed to preserve, rather than replace, their reservation households.[3]

From 1940 to 1980, men maintain some cultural activities even when they worked away from home. The loss of some cultural activities started when thousands of boys were sent to boarding schools away from their families. Many boys begin to doubt the creation narratives and cultural knowledge. Some boys started to accept and believe in Christian stories at the expense of the creation narratives. Historically, children learned Diné cultural knowledge from the family. While some families continue to teach their children this knowledge, some do not.

As men and women work constantly, the child's education is dependent on schools. Several schools on the reservation teach Diné history, culture, and language. Often, these schools teach cultural topics as electives and are secondary to the major subjects of math, science, social studies, and English. Many Diné men work, and many do not have the time to teach their child the cultural stories as much. Some do teach those stories, but not everyone. Consequently, some Diné men are working and not at home with the family. Many families spend most of their time at work or away from home.

Family support is part of Diné masculinities. Most Diné men work to support the family's wellness. Does working to ensure family prosperity equate to past elements of Diné masculinities? Some Diné children do not learn their clans. They learn very little or no cultural knowledge. Some children are not learning these stories because for the most part few individuals have the time and knowledge to tell them. Diné masculinities are shifting toward work-centered lives.

Third, some Diné men use drugs and alcohol. Historically, Diné men did not drink or ingest alcohol or mind-altering drugs. In the twenty-first century, some Diné men drink alcohol and/or use drugs to escape from the daily grind of life. The most common drug used is alcohol. Frank Mitchell, in *Navajo Blessingway Singer*, describes how alcohol was part of the male activity in the early part of the twentieth century.

> Afterwards, we got to talking, and they said that just a short distance back on the road there was a saloon. You see, it was off the reservation. Somebody said, "let's go over there and get something to drink and have a little fun." When that was suggested, of course a lot of them wanted to go. I was included, so I went over there on foot. It was not very far away, and we walked over to that saloon to buy something to drink. When we got there, of course, each one brought what he could afford. Some bought small bottles, others got big bottles. I bought a gallon jug, a clay one. I got that gallon of whiskey and some small bottles besides. We came back to camp, and of course we started drinking and talking and having a good time. We treated one another and kept on all night long.[4]

Mitchell indulged in the social atmosphere of drinking. In fact, many Diné men since the middle part of the nineteenth century participated in the social setting of alcohol consumption.

Clinical anthropologist Martin D. Topper examined Diné male adolescents to gain a better understanding of drinking as an expression of status. He found young males drank both for social cohesion and to escape problems. He also found children are introduced to drinking by the family. For example, ceremonies are a space where drinking takes place. Many in the extended family expect to support or help their relative during a healing ceremony, however some men aid the ceremony by pitching in to buy liquor. The "pitching in" exemplifies how young people participate and support a ceremony. Unfortunately, this particular example is not what their ancestors envisioned. As a result, alcohol has had a negative effect on some Diné families.

Topper connects a viable male image to alcohol in the earlier 1970s. He writes:

> This is a very serious problem facing many young Navajo men today. The problem arises from various sources, but underlying it is the fact that the young Navajo man is the one who suffers the most from the stresses of culture contact and culture change on the reservation.[5]

Young men in Topper's research drank to demonstrate their status among relatives and friends. While demonstrating a man's status is not new to any society let alone the Diné, drinking is an avenue for young men to "prove" their masculinity.

Alcohol consumption has led some men to act with a lack of concern for their families, particularly for their wives and children. Prior to colonization, Diné men acknowledged and fulfilled their role and responsibility as a hastiin in the extended family. Today, alcoholism and drug abuse have changed some Diné families. In the past, Diné masculinities had no connection to drug and alcohol abuse to show status. Male status was earned through hard work for the extended family, the clan, and the community. Male status was not about "showing off" to other men, but rather demonstrating to families the ability to work, protect, and serve them, their relatives, and their community. It appears that has changed for some Diné families and communities.

Fourth, emotional detachment from the family, the clan, and the community is prevalent. Not all Diné men are emotionally detached from their families, clans, and communities, but a large number are, and it affects their lives and Diné communities. For each individual man, the range of emotions depends on his coping skills. Some men will drink to handle their emotional detachment while others do something else.

Kunitz and Levy, in *Drinking, Conduct Disorder, and Social Change: Navajo Experiences*, argue alcohol abuse increases the rate of domestic violence, conduct disorder, suicide, and homicide. These consequences are significant because some families are suffering tremendously. Kunitz and Levy conclude young Diné men are more vulnerable to strains within Diné communities than are women, who have a more secure place.[6] They explain that this tension between men and women is not induce by American culture, but rather has always been a part of Diné communities. They cite the story of the separation of sexes in the third world and connect the historical interaction between the Pueblos and the Diné to the idea Diné men are more vulnerable to strains. Kunitz and Levy write:

> After the Navajos arrived in the Southwest, their society underwent several major economic transitions that affected the relative status of women. During a period of intense interaction with matrilineal Pueblo societies, which lasted from about 1690 to 1770, the Navajos adopted irrigation agriculture and developed a system of matrilineal descent that elevated women's status considerably. By 1830, the Navajos were obtaining over half of their subsistence from pastoral pursuits, and raiding for livestock had become common. Pastoralism is virtually always a male-managed affair, as are raiding and warfare. Just as male dominance was challenged during the period of intense contact with the Pueblos, so men struggled to attain the influence they felt they deserved once they came to manage the larger flocks and herds and to lead raiding parties in the years before their removal to a reservation.[7]

Diné oral history counters this stance on Diné and Pueblo cultural exchange. Diné and Pueblo cultural exchange did occur, however the narratives point to the fact that Diné men and women have always had a complementary partnership. Diné men did not dominate women, and cultural exchange was a two-way street. Diné culture did not borrow all of their culture from other communities. Other Native communities learned from Diné peoples, just as Diné peoples learned from them.

Kunitz and Levy take the approach that young Diné men cannot deal with stresses and strains. While some Diné men are abusing drugs and alcohol, many other men do not. The socioeconomic problems in Diné communities are symptoms of the fact that men are having problems coping with the physical and emotional responsibility. A Diné way of life is dependent on men who are integral to the prosperity and happiness in families. This lack of accountability and emotional stability by some men shows in male-female relationships.

Relationships between Diné men and women can be happy and harmonious, but also tense and harsh. Some Diné men act negatively toward Diné women. This attitude of male chauvinism is a fifth change in Diné masculinities.

The attitude of male dominance can be seen in parts of Diné communities but more so in the political arena. In 1998, LeNora Fulton ran for president of the Navajo Nation. She was heavily scrutinized. Many Diné peoples told Fulton the presidency is men's work and tradition must be followed. The tradition the people referred to was the idea that women should not lead. Diné men and women often cite the same narrative to bar women from political leadership:

> The Navajo have a legend about a woman leader. Her name was 'Asdzą́ą́ Naatáani (Woman Chief). She was the queen of her people in the underworld before the Navajos came to this land. Her authority was mostly over women and girls. She became lax in her authority, especially in regard to moral principles, thus making it easy for other women to become loose in their morals... There were many quarrels between the men and women over who was to support whom. The women said they did not need men to support them and this made the men angry. They decided to leave the women all to themselves and to make a new home far across a big sea. In time, life became hard for both sexes, but the queen and her daughter remained stubborn and would do nothing to bring the sexes back together. Finally, after four years, an old wise owl advised them there would be no more Dine'é if they continued with their foolishness. This made them admit that they were wrong, and ever since the men have taken over as rulers. My people have this story in mind when they criticize a woman leader. They say there will be confusion within the tribe whenever a Navajo woman takes office.[8]

This narrative is a variation on the interpretation, yet some people fail to recognize both men and women are needed for continuance. More often, the story is convenient as an excuse to keep women from the chief executive position. The current government structure is based on a Western democratic process; it is similar to the United States and other Western republics where men fill the majority of leadership positions.

The Diné creation narratives teach the people how men and women worked together to achieve sustainability. The stories teach the people how tradition was created and how it must be followed. Many cultures and peoples have influenced Diné traditions and politics. Diné peoples often equate the two even though the creation narratives distinguish the two. The two are not the same, but the separation of the sexes story is used to interpret tradition and politics in the same manner; men are to lead, and women cannot.

Diné lineage is traced through the mother, father, mother's father, and father's father. Land use rights, property and livestock rights, and the primary care of the household and children are historically the realm of Diné women. A Diné man can move in with his wife's family and help his in-laws. He does not entirely abandon his own biologically mother and father, but his new responsibility is with his wife and her family. In the twenty-first century, this cultural rule is arbitrarily followed, and many young men do not live with their wife's family.

Furthermore, some young and older men do not want their wives or girlfriends to be in a higher status position than them. Diné women are relegated to the domestic realm. Past Diné leadership was based on experience and cultural knowledge, not on gender or the sexes.

A sixth change is the American education system. Thousands of Diné men have graduated from colleges and universities. While knowledge and skills learned in colleges and universities helps both the individual and Diné peoples overall, the education attained is radically different than the knowledge and skills learned by their ancestors. Diné education is based on communal work and familial connections, learning a Diné matrix, and striving to live life based on SNBH. Attaining an American education excludes some Diné men from learning a Diné way of life. Learning worldly knowledge and establishing new friendships and connections to people is positive, while other circumstances, such as environmental destruction and individualistic greed, make Diné communities no different than the United States.

The number of Diné men graduating with associate, bachelor, and master's degrees is growing but still small. A fairly large number of Diné men do graduate from high school and enter the job market or join the military. Those choices have changed men's lifestyles. For some, work and/or the military helps discipline them, while for other men it creates doubt and confusion.

Western education is significant for Diné communities. This change has both a positive and negative experience. Some college educated Diné men are using Western knowledge to improve their way of life and communities, while others indulge in their own selfish motivations. Having a college education also affects relationships between men and women, and primarily, it has been a positive experience for college educated Diné men and women, although negative experiences do exist. How do Diné men feel when women are yearning to be leaders and earning higher household income? Relationships between Diné men and women are dissimilar. Some couples will be happy with very few challenges while other couples deal with daily, numerous problems. A discussion on Diné male-female relationships follows.

Relationships

In August 2006, Lynda Lovejoy came in second to incumbent President Joe Shirley in the Navajo presidential primary election. She was the first woman in Diné political history to face off against the incumbent in the general election for Navajo president. Her second place finish was a big surprise to numerous Navajo Nation council delegates and many in the Navajo general public. She lost the general election in November 2006 by over four thousand votes. She ran again in 2010 and lost the general election by over three thousand votes. Her public running for the highest political office brings to the forefront a discussion of Diné women as leaders in tribal government and the status of relationships between Diné women and men.

The Navajo Times, the independent weekly newspaper of the Navajo Nation, ran an online poll asking if there was any reason for a woman not to lead the Navajo Nation. A large number of people said gender did not matter, but rather the person's stances on the issues or how the candidate can help the people and nation. The assumption is Diné communities, particularly Diné men, respect the idea of women as leaders. However, not all Diné men feel this way.

The number of Diné women who have a college degree is higher than men due to the number of Navajo women attending college, graduate schools, and professional schools.[9] Behavioral studies and statistics also show domestic violence, alcohol abuse, depression, homicide, and other socioeconomic problems have risen. Based on these statistics, Diné men and women have challenging lives. The question becomes, how do these statistics reflect in the social and personal relationships?

Steve Allison offers his perspective on the notion of Diné men respecting Diné women:

> Respect for the female gender is a part of the Navajo traditional teachings. You are taught to respect your mothers, sisters, aunts, grandmother, etc. in Navajo culture because they gave birth to you, and these people are "who you are." However, I think most Navajo men are under the age of thirty-five. These young men are assimilated and not taught traditionally. Therefore, I think the majority of Navajo men do not respect Navajo women. This is evident in the instability of our young Navajos today.[10]

Brian Erickson, Phillip Lester, Randy Thompson, and Ken Lee counter Allison's view. Erickson says, "In general, I do believe Navajo men respect Navajo women. I have several friends who have been with their wives/lady friends for several years. They've had their troubled times but continue to share their lives with each other."[11] Lee says, "I believe the majority do respect Navajo women. Being a maternal society has influenced our feelings toward Navajo women."[12] Thompson expands on this perspective: "In Navajo traditional teaching Navajo women are very important because they are the ones bringing new lives to this world. According to the Navajo tradition, White Bead Woman came to this world as a powerful female. She started life. She was one of the Holy person (spirit)."[13]

According to several of the men, the lack of respect is based on age and generation. Scott Gordon believes it depends on age. He feels older Diné men are very respectful. Younger men are losing their identity, picking up a "new" culture, not knowing their relations, and displaying an aggressive behavior toward women. Barry Ryan also believes the younger generation does not value Diné women. He cites domestic abuse, drug use, and overall negativity on the reservation as evidence. Albert Burns thinks drugs, alcohol, and no discipline is the reason why some Diné men do not value Diné women. John Brown believes these men are not taught the proper way to treat women. He says:

Navajo men still respect Navajo women. As a Diné you are taught to be a good husband, father, son, etc…in the sweat lodge during puberty. You are told that you are from a woman. You are reminded of your mothers, sisters, grandmothers, etc. In this way, Navajo men still respect Navajo women. However, today many Navajo 'men' who were not taught these ways degrade women, they use women for one thing only and leave. They learned to disrespect the sacred bonds of love, marriage, and etc.[14]

Frank Begay offers a similar perspective to Brown's:

Some men will respect Navajo women, but there are those who don't, because of lack of understanding of the values of K'é and the clans. If we understand the values of a Diné woman, then the abuse can be lessened. But if we don't teach this to our children then when will this disrespect of Diné women stop? The woman is the home; she is the one that provides warmth, love and care. The woman is the child bearer, and for that she is to be revered. She brings life into the world. She brings love and warmth when everything seems bleak. She will restore the beauty in life. But an uneducated man about Diné women will do as he pleases.[15]

Diné relationships are a cornucopia of mixed feelings and thoughts. In the creation narratives, Diné men and women worked together to make life— iiná—without both working together, life is stagnant and imbalanced.

Historically, families arranged marriages between men and women. When it was time for a son to marry, the families considered a mate from an upstanding family. Anthropologist Gladys A. Reichard describes the scenario:

The father of the boy takes the initiative rather than his mother's brother… The matter is talked over in family council, and in choosing a wife for a son the father's voice is final and may override that of the maternal uncle, whereas the opinion of the girl's maternal uncle may take precedence over her father's or even over her own. Now let us suppose a girl is agreed upon, the proposal is made and accepted and the marriage takes place. Then it may be that the girl's family has also a son whom they will later marry to the sister of their son-in-law. Now in the first family there are a number of unmarried children, and the second family may know of mates for them although not in the immediate family, nevertheless they will be clan members, and mutual influence will be exerted to have them seek mates from the first family. And so it goes until we have an intricate network of clan and family alliances which is so complex that it defies any attempt to discover whether the affiliations are due primarily to desire for clan or family union or whether they are due merely to proximity of habitat.[16]

Marriages are arranged so clan rules can be followed properly and to determine which families are trustworthy. Arranged marriages are so rarely done in the twenty-first century. Most Diné men and women date and choose whom they will marry. Several of the men believe because of the lost of cultural teachings, problems have come about in relationships. For instance, Frank Begay says,

The negative side to this is just the opposite; people don't care who they date, clan sisters/brothers and so forth. They are related to each other, and they still go out. Sometimes, sad to say, there are some guys/men out there who don't care about the essence and beauty of the female, and they will abuse them; they will cheat and hit and sometimes even kill their girlfriends/wives over stupid little things.[17]

Bruce Jackson concurs with Begay.

There is too much coming and going in relationships. There are hardly any Navajo couples that married whether it be traditional Navajo or not. There is a trail of broken homes, hurt children and loved ones following Navajo men and women that cohabit before they ever get married, especially children out of wedlock really breaks my heart.[18]

John Brown has an interesting and observant perspective on Diné relationships. He believes American thought has altered historical Diné perspectives on what marriage should be. He believes both Diné men and women follow too much of an American perspective on relationships, and both need to learn historical roles for Diné men and women. He says:

Contemporary relationships between Navajo men and women are for the most part dictated by Western views of marriage or relationships. For example, Navajo women want to be romanced and showered with gifts as a token of love, etc. However, they do not fulfill the traditional roles of being a Navajo woman. Similarly, Navajo men spend too much time trying to please their women or to keep them happy and overlook the traditional teachings of being a Navajo male in law.[19]

Brian Erickson offers a counter perspective to Begay, Jackson, and Brown.

I view contemporary relationships between Navajo men and Navajo women as optimistic. I believe in any working relationship, there is a lot of collaboration taking place. Each individual must respect each other's opinion no matter if it's negative or positive. There is no guarantee in any relationship; it depends on both parties, if they want to make it work.[20]

David Francis discusses how some Diné men and women get tired or discouraged if they meet other Diné men and women who are related by clan. He says they just pick someone who is not Diné to settle down with in life. Steve Allison has seen some exogamous marriages work, but he feels most have problems. He says:

So in Navajo-non-Navajo relationships, the non-Navajo man resides with the female's Navajo family. These non-Navajo men become "hadaane" (in-law) to the Navajo families. I have seen some of these relations work on the Navajo reservation with non-Navajo hadaane, but I think most of these relationships don't work. This is probably because of the differences in values, religion, etc. Once again, the number of half-breed children you see on the Navajo reservation with single mothers is common. A lot of the time too, non-Navajo men do not respect the customs, traditions, and values of Navajo families they become a part of. This causes a lot of problems too."[21]

In the twenty-first century, more Diné men and women are marrying non-Diné persons. In the 2010 US Census, over forty thousand individuals identify themselves as a combination of Diné and one or more other races. Intermarriages are common for Native Americans.

Sociologists Gary D. Sandefur and Trudy McKinnell in 1986 examined American Indian intermarriage and found American Indians are the least racially endogamous. They conclude:

> Indians in "Indian" states—those with traditionally higher concentrations of Indians—are more endogamous than those in non-Indian states. Indians are, however, more likely to intermarry with whites in Indian states than in non-Indian states, after adjustments are made for the number of men and women in the different racial groups...Of the three racial groups considered in this analysis, intermarriage is most prevalent among the American Indian population.[22]

Intermarriages and dating other races and ethnicities is part of Diné life and all Native communities. It is not a new trend.

Historically, Diné peoples married non-Diné peoples such as Jemez, Zuni, Hopi, and others. In the Diné clanship system, several clans such as the Naakaii dine'é and Nóóda'í dine'é are formed based on marriages with the Mexican and Ute peoples. By intermarrying other Native peoples, the clanship system has vitality. In the twenty-first century, intermarriages create an atmosphere some Diné peoples feel threatens the integrity of the culture and way of life. For example, Steve Allison says, "There are a lot of divorces among Navajos today because a significant amount of Navajos deviated from the traditional values and teachings."[23] Frank Begay concurs:

> Since we are so far fledged from our values and teachings, we are dating our enemy! If we are to take our grandmothers teachings seriously for a moment, then this is what is happening. Today, we just go along with the actions of our children because we think differently than how our parents and grandparents thought. It has become a personal choice, why do you think in the old days, Diné parents arranged marriages for their sons? To avoid all this.[24]

Several men feel dating and/or marrying a non-Diné woman is up to the individuals involved, but they feel challenges to such a union are inevitable. For instance, Troy Mann says, "There will be cultural barriers. I believe in order for this to happen, the Navajo would have to be really educated to fulfill all expectations to the non-Navajo."[25] Lee agrees with Mann. He believes it will be difficult for interracial relationships to be happy and successful, but it depends immensely on the two people involved.

Michael Wagner extends this view by discussing the impact of colonization on how Diné men and women view relationships and/or marriages with non-Diné peoples. He states:

> If it works, that's great. However there should be some discussion involving children of such things as home site leases (e.g., land holding, land tenure), being an enrolled tribal member, blood quantum issues that affect cultural identity, language acquisition (e.g., being bilingual), type of schooling desired, etc. At one time, prior to our colonization by the US, Diné had a system for adopting new clans, consisting of people from different tribes and backgrounds. The BIA system, presently in place, promotes a very different way of addressing diversity with it "blood quantum" system. These colonial practices will only negatively interfere with Navajo people dating or marrying outside the tribe.[26]

John Brown also brings up the issue of interracial relationships in terms of how people view races and ethnicities. He says:

> In many cases I have heard Navajo women say, "I can't find the right Navajo man so I married a white guy." That is problematic. There are plenty of Navajo men around who are good mates. Instead, I think these women internalize oppressed thoughts leading them to think that only white men are better or black men are better in bed, etc...Later in life, many of these same women find that they fell in love or married for the wrong reasons. Sure if they can maintain and honor the Diné way of life and still marry outside, then there is no problem. That is, if a Navajo woman dates or marry a non-Navajo for the right reason than I have no problem with it. However, often times, women later in life find that it is harder to preserve this relationship especially when cultural and religious differences arise.[27]

Both Wagner and Brown's perspectives bring up critical questions on the impact of colonization on relationships. For instance, can a Diné man or woman maintain their culture and language if they marry a non-Diné man or woman? How do Diné men and women maintain the culture and language in a mixed relationship?

Adam Blake is married to a non-Diné woman and is frowned upon by Diné women when he tells them that. Blake admits he did not consciously want to marry a non-Diné woman, but he does feel it is important to be in a relationship with a Diné woman to maintain traditions and rituals. In his marriage, his non-Diné wife encourages him to teach his child the culture and language. In fact, both of them are committed to maintaining Diné culture.

This brings up even more questions; such as how do Diné peoples assess cultural continuance? Is it by the number of fluent language speakers or by how many Diné men and women marry other Diné men and women? One definite fact is relationships between Diné men and non-Diné women will continue.

Paul Yazzie describes a distinct pride among Diné peoples to marry within the nation. Brian Erickson disagrees. He says, "I don't have any negative feelings about Navajo women dating other non-Navajo men. We all have our different perspectives of a successful relationship. Just depends on how we have been raised and our expectation of life goals."[28] Randy Thompson concurs with Erickson: "There is nothing wrong with a Navajo man dating and marrying a non-Diné woman. They bring beautiful people into this world."[29] Matthew Billison offers a thoughtful and sensitive perspective on Diné and non-Diné relationships:

> I have always been told that it is more appropriate for Navajo women to marry Navajo men, due to traditional and cultural reasons, that there is a specific role for a man and a woman. I think Navajo women should marry Navajo men, but it's the choice of the Navajo woman. I have friends and relatives who have great relationships and marriages outside of Navajo.[30]

How do Diné women feel? Conversing with two women, they offer similar and different views.

Andrea Yazzie, twenty-four years old, has an optimistic perspective when it comes to intermarriage. Her view is that if a Diné man is married to, or dating, a non-Diné woman based on love and affection, then it's fine. She feels a "true" loving, compassionate, generous, and thoughtful interracial couple should be seen in awe for having found love in life. She does, however, feel some interracial couples do not come together for good reasons. She says, "I have a problem when I see a couple together who are a mixed race couple where they use it as revenge, status, or as a way to fulfill a fantasy of doing what is exotic, different, and unique than staying within their norm."[31]

Vicky Charley, twenty-five years old, feels Diné men do not value Diné women when it comes to relationships:

> I think it depends on what "kind" of Navajo man you are talking about. If you are speaking of a Navajo male who has been raised with some idea of Navajo cultural values, then yes, a Navajo male has respect for Navajo women. But, then again that respect in many cases is blurred. I think many Navajo men have found a hole that allows for them to take advantage of women as the source of money, shelter, food, and material goods. Currently, I have female family and friends who "have

a man" in their lives, but he usually is a male who is taking advantage of them materially, and thus in a sense is disrespecting her.[32]

Some Diné women feel some Diné men do have respect for them, but others do not, and they feel they lack the cultural knowledge to know how to do so.

Relationships between Diné men and women are more complicated in the twenty-first century. Many factors affect the communication and well-balanced nature of companionship. Many young Diné people choose whom they date and marry. Arranged marriages are no longer a common practice, though a few families continue to do so. The choice of wanting to have a relationship with a Diné man or woman is a realistic experience for many in Diné communities. All thirty men believe it is important for a Diné man to marry a Diné woman to maintain traditions, culture, and language. Steve Allison frames what many men think on the idea of marrying and having a relationship with a Diné woman:

> It is important to have common values with the person you are marrying so that your chance of a successful marriage increases. I have heard that if you want to increase your chances of a successful marriage, marry someone with the same values (traditions, culture, language) and religion as you. Differences in values and religions cause a lot of problems in relationships, especially when deciding what values and religion the children are going to be raised with. Many marriages end in divorce because there are just too many problems that arise from the differences in values and religion. Therefore, common traditions, culture, and language are a big factor in deciding who to marry. In Navajo, you are taught that marriage is for life unlike American society, where divorce is very common.[33]

Brian Erickson also believes in Diné men marrying Diné women. He says, "You would want to strengthen your Navajo culture environment by learning from each other as you grow together, and share your knowledge with your children, families, and friends so they can keep the Navajo culture alive."[34] John Brown is passionate for this concern:

> I return to an earlier statement that only by maintaining our language and cultural traditions (not the fry bread or the biil dress only but all that defines our unique identity as Diné) can we hope to give something to our children that they can be proud of. Otherwise, our children will become the same as everyone else, which was the goal of the founding fathers of America (one large melting pot). If we are to maintain our identity, sovereignty, our rights, then we need to do it and not talk about. I believe that only by being with a Navajo woman who respects and honors those values will it happen. Sure non-Navajos can do it too, but they have to know the traditions, language, etc.[35]

Yazzie and Charley have similar views. Yazzie sums up her take on relationships:

> There is this one poem by Sherman Alexie in his book *One Stick Song* where he talks about how he went to this conference award show and there were all these good, educated Indian men that were married or with non-native women, and at that moment he realized that he would do justice to his culture and the valuable native women by taking care of and marrying a native woman. In that poem, I really felt that to make a conscious choice and effort to do that, when the time is right, to show and display the value of our culture and women is a good choice. It may not be the choice for everyone, but if the majority embraces it not as bias, prejudice, and a negative thing but as something worth preserving, I think that we all as indigenous people would be better off.[36]

For the thirty men and the two women, having a relationship with a Diné woman or man is important to maintaining the vitality of a Diné way of life. However, the choice is left up to the individual, not the family or the community.

What becomes of this approach in the future is uncertain, but more Diné men and women are dating and marrying non-Diné, and at the same time more Diné men and women are dating and marrying other Diné. It seems both men and women want to date and marry other Diné, though complications do arise during courtship, and determining whether people remain together or not is based on the individuals' circumstances not necessarily family arrangement. For most of the men, they are willing to be in an endogamous relationship to help maintain a Diné way of life, but they do not view exogamous relationships as wrong.

Conclusion

American culture impacts Diné men. Diné communities allow individuality and autonomy, yet community needs are always paramount. Living by one's self and doing things on one's own was unheard of two hundred-plus years ago. Some Diné men are concerned for their immediate family rather than the community's well-being in the twenty-first century. Some Diné men focus their attention on work and not on their family. Some Diné men for most of the twentieth century worked and taught the stories, prayers, songs, and other cultural knowledge to their children; smaller numbers do so today. Fewer people live life based on SNBH. Alcohol and drugs command some Diné men; they abuse these substances, and the consequences are in all areas of Diné communities. Before alcohol and drugs, Diné men were emotionally healthy. For some men, unwellness started when they abused alcohol and/or drugs. Some men are emotionally detached from their family and friends. They live challenging and in some cases debilitating lives.

On a positive note, more men have earned college degrees. While they are learning the knowledge and skills necessary to succeed in American society, fewer men are learning the cultural knowledge of their ancestors. Even then, Diné masculinities have similar experiences, such as love for others and maintaining complicated clanships and relationships similar to those in the past, regardless of how or what changes occur. Diné masculinities are different from the past, and this difference has led to Diné men understanding their masculinity through an American lens.

Diné relationships have also been altered. Many Diné men emphasize how much more complicated relationships are between men and women than ever before. In the past, Diné families arranged marriages for sons and daughters. In the twenty-first century, almost all Diné families do not arrange their children's marriage. Instead, men and women date to find a compatible mate. Some men and women ignore the clan rule and either date and/or marry a clan relative. For some men and women, they eventually discover many people are related to them, so they decide to marry a non-Diné.

Some Diné men do not value Diné women, yet others do in fact respect women. Brian Erickson says, "Relationships do have tumultuous times, yet the couple works at it to ensure they stay together."[37] Some Diné men also feel a Diné woman should not date and/or marry a non-Diné man. In general, many Diné men believe having a relationship with a Diné woman will help maintain traditions, culture, and the language.

Diné communities are diverse. All Diné men are different from one another. Most men are good individuals who respect women in general. They have friends and relatives who are battling their addictions to alcohol and/or drugs. Most men marry Diné women, though they do know of a relative or friend who married a non-Diné.

Many Diné men want a Diné way of life to continue and acknowledge problems do occur in their relationships. For most men, they work hard to maintain a harmonious partnership. All relationships seek harmony, and the men are trying diligently to achieve this with their partners. Exogamous marriages will continue as well as endogamous relationships. What the future holds is that Diné men and women will continue to live with the people and families they cherish and love, no matter the race, ethnicity, gender, class, and/or social standing.

7
Siihasin: Reflecting on Diné Masculinities

Siihasin in Diné means to reflect, ponder, and to think about the experience. Siihasin is part of the planning and learning process in life: nitsáhákees (thinking), nahat'á (planning), and iiná (living). In Diné, the four-part planning and learning process is tied to SNBH. SNBH is the land, the seasons, the cardinal directions, the stages of the day, the stages of life, and all other energies. Rex Lee Jim in "A Moment in My Life" supplies a personal perspective on SNBH. He writes:

> I immediately realized that in order for me to reach old age, the quality of my action in the moment was of utmost importance. Suddenly *sa* no longer meant old age in terms of years, *sa* came to mean quality. *Sa* is quality: quality of ever-improving spirituality, quality of physical growth, quality of social flexibility, and quality of mental processing. *Sa* is the quality of ever-moving human wellness, and therefore a process of a healthy and wealthy world. I have come to realize that those who reach old not only believe in quality, they also had a definite purpose in life and a definite plan to achieve it.[1]

Jim has a purposeful life. He is a planner, too. Frank Mitchell, in *Navajo Blessingway Singer: The Autobiography of Frank Mitchell, 1881-1967,* defines planner as a naat'áanii. According to Mitchell, naat'áanii is one who plans for the future. This person is not a leader or a headman or a king or a president or a dictator. The planner thinks of the future for the family and community.

In reflection, each man's life is similar in various ways, yet differing viewpoints frame their individuality and their relations. Diné men have experiences that are similar to, and different from, those of American men. Male performance does not play a significant role in what it means to be a hastiin, yet it is starting to influence Diné masculinities. While Diné men learn and follow American perspectives on masculinities, such as making your own life and displaying masculinity through sport and/or military participation, families and schools significantly influence Diné male development. Diné men combine an American attitude on masculinities with historical Diné male attributes. Diné men protect their families and loved ones. They believe a man must take responsibility for his own actions. Fatherhood does not necessarily establish masculinity, but if he provides for and protects his child, then he is a hastiin. Moreover, the ability to confront violence is another attribute of Diné masculinities.

Diné men are hunters, farmers, teachers, storytellers, traders, protectors, and healers. They frame masculinities by spirituality, social image, common lifestyle, and physical body. Also, a woman complements and completes a hastiin. In fact, without a Diné woman, a hastiin is not a full human being. Men live the principles of iiná—to live well, to know the history of the people and the Diyin Dine'é, to follow SNBH, to live with the four basic elements, to practice K'é and K'éí, and to speak the Diné language. Diné boys go through the kinaaldá to learn what it means to be a young man. They learn the stories, prayers, songs, and cultural knowledge. The attributes of historical Diné masculinities still live, but it is not universal among all Diné men.

The thirty men recognize colonization has altered Diné communities. A Diné man's concept of individuality has change. Some men are more work-centered than family-first, some men abuse drugs and alcohol, and some are emotionally detached from their families. Some men accept the notion of male dominance. Many Diné men are Western educated. Most Diné men believe they need to balance both American ideals of being a man with the historical attributes of a Diné matrix. More men are speaking English only, and fewer know the stories, prayers, and songs of the past. Each of the thirty men shows the degree of change to Diné masculinities.

Diné women are not dissimilar to men. Relationships between Diné men and women show how colonialism influences attitudes and beliefs. In the past, families arranged marriages for sons and daughters. In the twenty-first century, almost all families do not arrange their child's marriage. Almost all Diné men and women date to find a compatible mate. Some, in fact, ignore the clan rule to not date and marry a clan relative. Interracial marriages have increased in the last fifty years. Some of the thirty men feel a Diné woman should not date and/or marry a non-Diné man. Overall, most of the thirty Diné men believe having a relationship with a Diné woman will help maintain a Diné way of life.

While a Diné matrix continues, many characteristics of historical Diné thought are no longer known or practiced. Diné masculinities will continue to change with each generation, and ties to cultural teachings might loosen or grow tighter. While less cultural knowledge is taught to Diné children, a Diné matrix continues in a different form. Nonetheless, commonalities exist between the historical and present-day. The kinaaldá is still widely held for girls and at times for boys. Each Diné man represents the attributes of sustenance, responsibility, respect, hospitality, knowledge, and health. Representatively, present-day ideas and values impact how Diné men think, live, and act. Future studies will be necessary to monitor the impact and to find, hopefully not, if historical attributes of Diné masculinities are completely gone.

Implications

This study has several implications. It presents thirty personal perspectives and offers examples of what Diné men are thinking. While all the men in this study live fairly good lives, numerous Diné men do not. The thirty men can tell their life stories. Diné peoples can see how these thirty men maintain individual and autonomous Diné ways of life.

The first implication of this study is Diné men need to have a proactive life. Peter Walker describes one of his life's goals:

> I think helping our Diné people in our own way, by whatever means. Whether that be working to correct our mistakes, taking care of our children in a decent way, working for the tribe, or practicing our culture, we should be mindful on improving the lives of our people in some form of fashion through whatever contribution. I want to look back on my life knowing I contributed to the overall welfare of the Diné in some way.[2]

The proactive life Walker takes illustrates an effective way to confront change and the pressures of living in the United States.

A second implication is the realization some Diné men do not respect women and do not live up to the standards of their ancestors. Unfortunately, numerous Diné men are in prison, homeless, alcoholics, abuse women, jobless, or destitute. If a preponderance of Diné men is impaired, then Diné communities will continue to suffer. All of the thirty men live fairly good lives, but recognize that some Diné men are destitute and do not respect women.

Diné male respect is fundamental to resolving many socioeconomic problems facing Diné families. The deficiency of many Diné men is having a detrimental effect on all Diné communities. If the deficiency is not stopped and reversed, Diné communities will continue to have problems. This implication needs to be addressed by all families, and the testimonies of these thirty men can provide perspective in helping to develop strategies to counter this concern.

A third implication is the realization that Diné masculinities have significant differences from those of other American men and men around the world. Some of those significant differences include male development and masculine expression. Some Diné men grew up learning Diné cultural knowledge. Some of the thirty men believe Diné masculinities are expressed comprehensively in life, rather than through a basic approach. Generally, Diné masculinities have many similarities to American masculinities, yet several significant differences are evident.

A fourth implication is a development of strategies for successful leadership. Many Diné peoples feel there is a lack of leadership among men, and these thirty individuals can be examples of what changes are needed in leadership and how men can be effective leaders. Frank Begay says a Diné man is a leader when he sets goals for himself and his family and achieves them. The experiences of these men can serve as effective examples for boys and young men on how to be reliable leaders.

A fifth implication is the idea Diné masculinities are open-ended, rather than defined by a litmus test of historical characteristics. For instance, a Diné man is only Diné if he speaks the language, grew up on the reservation, knows how to herd sheep, or wears turquoise jewelry. This type of representation is representative of past Diné masculinities. Most of the men feel speaking the Diné language does not necessarily establish Diné masculinity. While speaking the language is important for Diné continuance, using language as a barrier to exclude some Diné peoples is unacceptable.

An open-ended approach to framing Diné masculinities creates a dilemma for men and Diné peoples. The dilemma is that language does and does not establish Diné identity. Language maintenance and revitalization is a concern and challenge for Diné peoples, yet the willingness to have a flexible perspective on Diné masculinities offers an effective way to live, otherwise disharmony or resentment will deteriorate Diné communities. All of the men adopt a flexible approach. Diné communities can learn how to be flexible to help restore Diné thought.

A sixth implication is creating good male role models. Colonization and globalization is both negative and positive, yet many families have negative stories of their husbands, boyfriends, brothers, uncles, and cousins dying young, beating up their wives or girlfriends, or abusing alcohol or drugs. The thirty men for the most part are able to overcome challenges and to have productive lives. While each man is not perfect in his decisions, indigenous men who are living very challenging lives can look at how each of these men overcame their obstacles. Throughout Diné history, role models are a part of leadership and families. The uncle on the maternal side of the family is the disciplinarian, but also a dependable figure for the family. While the grandmother is the central figure in the family, the uncle is a pillar of stability.

In this study, I wanted to find out how Diné men constructed and displayed their masculinities, and I discovered Diné masculinities have strains of historical attributes intermixed with American male concepts. Each of the thirty men live independent and different lives, but each is also interlinked with Diné thought. Some of the men learned a Diné way of life, while others did not. Each man's upbringing is different and the impact their families and Western education have had on their male development is fundamental to Diné masculinities.

Colonization has changed how Diné men think and act, though providing for and protecting the family remains a vital aspect of Diné masculinities. A historical Diné matrix mentions change, and these men are products of change. While many aspects of Diné communities are in terrible and debilitating conditions, Diné men can help rectify the problem. They must recognize the terrible conditions many families are in and use wise judgment to alleviate them. Diné men cannot take the high moral ground and say women should do the work. Both men and women are needed to improve the situation and rebuild the Navajo Nation where prosperity and well-being are paramount for all.

Diné men must live and practice the historical meaning of naat'áanii. Men must be planners, thinkers, and doers for the future. Diné communities will need men who can help and plan for family stability, community sustainability, and a nation's wellness. They will want men who are selfless and willing to have proactive lives. In the past, all Diné men were responsible to the community. Diné men can apply responsibility to community and family to help sustain the Navajo Nation. Diné men can relearn what it means to be a naat'áanii. It begins with one man, one hastiin.

Notes

Chapter 1. Introduction

[1] I use the term matrix instead of philosophy to describe Navajo thought. Native American philosopher Viola F. Cordova preferred the term matrix. For her, the term implied a web of related concepts. It is defined as something within which something else originates and takes its form. The term describes a web of perspectives and other influences to both individual and community. It serves as a foundation upon which all else hinges. Three basic concepts set a worldview: a description of the world, a description of what it is to be human in the world, and a description of the role of human in the world. A Navajo matrix follows these three basic concepts.

[2] Linda Tuhiwai Smith, *Decolonizing Methodologies: Research and Indigenous Peoples* (London: Zed Books Ltd, 1999), 145.

[3] Ibid., 151.

Chapter 2. Nitsáhákees: Thinking of Diné Masculinities

[1] "Walter Johnson," interview by author, Lukachukai, AZ, February 11, 2006.

[2] "Peter Walker," interview by author, Albuquerque, NM, August 2005.

[3] John R. Farella, *The Main Stalk: A Synthesis in Navajo Philosophy* (Albuquerque: University of New Mexico Press, 1984), 212.

[4] Wesley Thomas, "Navajo Cultural Constructions of Gender and Sexuality," in *Two-Spirit People: Native American Gender Identity, Sexuality, and Spirituality*, ed. Sue-Ellen Jacobs, Wesley Thomas, and Sabine Lang (Urbana, IL: University of Illinois Press, 1997), 156-173.

[5] Tim Edwards, *Cultures of Masculinity* (London: Routledge, 2006), 2.

[6] Michael Kimmel, "Global Masculinities: Restoration and Resistance," *Gender Policy Review*, November 2000.

[7] Ibid.

[8] Erving Goffman, *Stigma: Notes on the Management of Spoiled Identity* (Englewood Cliffs, NJ: Prentice Hall, 1963), 128.

[9] Kimmel, "Global Masculinities: Restoration and Resistance."

[10] Michael Messner, "Boyhood, Organized Sports, and the Construction of Masculinities," *Journal of Contemporary Ethnography* 18, no. 4 (1990): 416-444.

[11] Michael Kimmel, *Manhood in America: A Cultural History* (New York: The Free Press, 1996), 17.

[12] Warren Steinberg, *Masculinity: Identity Conflict and Transformation* (Boston: Shambhala, 1993), 21.

[13] Ibid., 64.

[14] Anne Gavanas, *Fatherhood Politics in the United States: Masculinity, Sexuality, Race, and Marriage* (Urbana, IL: University of Illinois Press, 2004), 25.

[15] Ibid., 34.

[16] Ibid., 52.

[17] Ibid., 31.

[18] bell hooks, *The Will to Change: Men, Masculinity, and Love* (New York: Atria Books, 2004), 82.

[19] Ibid., 187-188.

[20] Brendon Hokowhitu, "Tackling Maori Masculinity: A Colonial Genealogy of Savagery and Sport," *The Contemporary Pacific* 16, no. 2 (Fall 2004): 269.

[21] Kim Anderson, *A Recognition of Being: Reconstructing Native Womanhood* (Toronto, Ontario: Sumach Press, 2000), 69.

[22] Ibid., 91-92.

[23] Ty P. Kawika Tengan, "Hale Mua: (En)Gendering Hawaiian Men" (Ph.D. diss., University of Hawai'i, August 2003), 77.

Chapter 3. History of Diné Masculinities

[1] Ethelou Yazzie, ed., *Navajo History Volume I* (Chinle, AZ: Rough Rock Press, 1971).

[2] Some Navajo versions of the story do not mention of a second visit by the twins to see their father. This version is borrowed from *Navajo History Volume I* and various individuals who discuss this story.

[3] In Navajo culture, people are not supposed to discuss death or come into connect with funerary objects or items.

[4] Tiana Bighorse, *Bighorse the Warrior* (Tucson, AZ: The University of Arizona Press, 1990), xxiv.

[5] David M. Brugge, "Navajo Archaeology: A Promising Past," in *The Archaeology of Navajo Origins*, ed. Ronald H. Towner (Salt Lake City, UT: University of Utah Press, 1996), 270-71.; Peter Iverson, *Diné: A History of the Navajos* (Albuquerque, NM: University of New Mexico Press, 2002), 18-19.

[6] David E. Wilkins, *The Navajo Political Experience* (Lanham, MD: Rowman & Littlefield Publishers, Inc., 2003).

[7] Lynn Robinson Bailey, *Indian Slave Trade in the Southwest: A Study of Slave-Taking and the Traffic in Indian Captives* (Los Angeles, CA: Westernlore Press, 1966).; Frank McNitt, *Navajo Wars: Military Campaigns, Slave Raids, and Reprisals* (Albuquerque, NM: University of New Mexico Press, 1972).

[8] LaVerne Harrell Clark, *They Sang for Horses: The Impact of the Horse on Navajo and Apache Folklore* (Boulder, CO: University Press of Colorado, 2001).

[9] Ruth M. Underhill, *The Navajos* (Norman, OK: University of Oklahoma Press, 1956).

[10] "Mrs. Nez-Bah," interview by Tom Ration, August 27, 1968, tape 144, side 1, transcript, American Indian Oral History Project Collection, Center for Southwest Research, Albuquerque, NM.; Gladys A. Reichard, *Social Life of the Navajo Indians, with some attention to minor ceremonies* (New York: Columbia University Press, 1928).

[11] "Anonymous," interview by Martin D. Topper, December 12, 1970, tape 757, side 1, American Indian Oral History Project Collection, Center for Southwest Research, Albuquerque, NM.

[12] Iverson, *Diné: A History of the Navajos*, 23.

[13] "Anonymous," American Indian Oral History Project Collection, Center for Southwest Research, Albuquerque, NM.

[14] "Bob Manuelito," interview by Tom Ration, February 1969, tape 288, reel mfm 2, American Indian Oral History Project Collection, Center for Southwest Research, Albuquerque, NM.

[15] Frank McNitt, *Navajo Wars: Military Campaigns, Slave Raids, and Reprisals* (Albuquerque, NM: University of New Mexico Press, 1972).; David

M. Brugge, *Navajos in the Catholic Church Records of New Mexico, 1694-1875* (Tsaile, AZ: Navajo Community College Press, 1985).

[16] Iverson, *Diné: A History of the Navajos*, 26.

[17] New Mexico Department of Cultural Affairs, "The Story of Bosque Redondo," 2005.

[18] "Treaty Between The United States of America and The Navajo Tribe of Indians," 25 July 1868.

[19] New Mexico Department of Cultural Affairs, "The Story of Bosque Redondo," 2005.

[20] Iverson, *Diné: A History of the Navajos*, 64-65.; Luci Tapahonso, "In 1864," in *Saanii Dahataal: The Women are Singing* (Tucson, AZ: University of Arizona Press, 1993).

[21] Charlotte J. Frisbie and David P. McAllester, eds., *Navajo Blessingway Singer: The Autobiography of Frank Mitchell, 1881-1967* (Albuquerque, NM: University of New Mexico Press, 2003).

[22] Frisbie and Mcallester, eds., *Navajo Blessingway Singer*, 46.

[23] Ibid., 78.

[24] "Cozy Stanley Brown," in *Navajos and World War II*, ed. Broderick H. Johnson (Tsaile, AZ: Navajo Community College Press, 1977), 61.; Iverson, *Diné: A History of the Navajos*, 183.

[25] Carl Voegelin, Flo Voegelin, and Noel Schutz, "The Language Situation in Arizona as Part of the Southwest Culture Area," in *Studies in Southwestern Ethnolinguistics: Meaning and History in the Languages of the American Southwest*, ed. Dell Hymes with William E. Bittle (The Hague Paris, France: Mouton & Co, 1967), 403-451.

[26] Navajo Tribal Council requests, NAPR, Navajo Area Office.; Iverson, *Diné: A History of the Navajos*, 189.

[27] Robert A. Roessel, Jr., *Navajo Education, 1948-1978: Its Progress and Its Problems* (Rough Rock, AZ: Navajo Curriculum Center, Rough Rock Demonstration School, 1979), 18-19.

[28] Ibid., 18-19.; Iverson, *Diné: A History of the Navajos*, 193.

[29] *Navajo Times*, January 7, 1971.; Iverson, *Diné: A History of the Navajos*, 248.

[30] Donald A. Grinde and Bruce E. Johansen, *Ecocide of Native America: Environmental Destruction of Indian Lands and Peoples* (Santa Fe, NM: Clear Light Publishers, 1995).; Iverson, *Diné: A History of the Navajos*, 219.;

Timothy Benally, interview, Navajo Uranium Workers Oral History Project, Doug Brugge, coordinator, PIPC.

[31] Iverson, *Diné: A History of the Navajos*, 219.

[32] Grinde and Johansen, *Ecocide of Native America*, 208-209.; Iverson, *Diné: A History of the Navajos*, 219.

[33] Stephen J. Kunitz and Jerrold E. Levy, *Drinking, Conduct Disorder, and Social Change: Navajo Experience* (Oxford: Oxford University Press, 2000).

[34] Martin D. Topper, "Drinking as an Expression of Status: Navajo Male Adolescents," in *Drinking Behavior Among Southwestern Indians: An Anthropological Perspectives*, eds. Jack O. Waddell & Michael W. Everett (Tucson, AZ: The University of Arizona Press, 1980), 103-147.

[35] Kunitz and Levy, *Drinking, Conduct Disorder, and Social Change*, 25-27.

[36] Eric Henderson, Stephen J. Kunitz, and Jerrold E. Levy, "The Origins of Navajo Youth Gangs," *American Indian Culture and Research Journal* 23, no. 3 (1999): 243-264.

[37] Trib Choudhary, *Navajo Nation Data from US Census 2000* (Window Rock, AZ: Division of Economic Development, Navajo Nation, 2002).

[38] Jerry Kammer, "New, Unifying Ritual: 'Rezball,'" *Arizona Republic*, September 19, 1993.; Iverson, *Diné: A History of the Navajos*, 308-310.

Chapter 4. Foundational Image of Diné Masculinities

[1] See Father Berard Haile, Washington Matthews, Gladys Reichard, and others who have written on various Diné healing ceremonies such as the Night Way and Enemy Way.

[2] Ernest Harry Begay, "Navajo Summer Storytelling" (storytelling session, Arizona State University, Tempe, AZ, September 10, 2005).

[3] Herbert J. Benally, "Navajo Philosophy of Learning and Pedagogy," in *Journal of Navajo Education* XII, no. 1 (Fall 1994): 23-31.

[4] Gary Witherspoon, *Language and Art in the Navajo Universe* (Ann Arbor, MI: The University of Michigan Press, 1977), 20.

[5] Ibid., 32.

[6] Miranda J. Haskie, "Preserving a Culture: Practicing the Navajo Principles of Hózhǫ́ dóó K'é" (Ph.D. diss., Fielding Graduate Institute, 2002).

[7] Ibid., 33.

[8] Ibid., 33; Trudy Griffin-Pierce, *Earth is my Mother, Sky is my Father: Space, Time, and Astronomy in Navajo Sandpainting* (Albuquerque: University of New Mexico Press, 1992).

[9] Miranda J. Haskie, "Preserving a Culture: Practicing the Navajo Principles of Hózhǫ́ dóó K'é" (Ph.D. diss., Fielding Graduate Institute, 2002); Wilson Aronlith, Jr., *Foundation of Navajo Culture* (Tsaile, AZ: Diné College, 1992).

[10] Begay, "Navajo Summer Storytelling," September 10, 2005.

[11] Ibid.

[12] Gary Witherspoon, *Navajo Kinship and Marriage* (Chicago: University of Chicago Press, 1975).

[13] This is a personal observation and discussion with numerous Diné people, relatives, and friends. Very few are done each year although there is a resurgence going on among Diné families.

[14] Maureen Trudelle Schwarz, *Molded in the Image of Changing Woman: Navajo Views on the Human Body and Personhood* (Tucson: The University of Arizona Press, 1997), 159.

[15] Begay, "Navajo Summer Storytelling," September 10, 2005.

[16] Father Berard Haile, *Origin Legends of the Navajo Enemyway* (New Haven, CT: Yale University Press, 1938), 105; Schwarz, *Molded in the Image of Changing Woman: Navajo Views on the Human Body and Personhood*, 167.

[17] Begay, "Navajo Summer Storytelling," September 10, 2005.

[18] Gladys Reichard, *Navaho Religion: A Study of Symbolism* (New York: Pantheon, 1950), 39.

Chapter 5. Iiná: Diné Male Perspectives

[1] US Bureau of the Census. *The American Indian and Alaska Native Population: 2010, 2010 Census Briefs*. Prepared by the US Department of Commerce Economics and Statistics Adminstration, Bureau of the Census. Washington, DC, 2012.

[2] Ibid.

[3] Trib Choudhary, *Navajo Nation Data from US Census 2000* (Window Rock, AZ: Division of Economic Development, Navajo Nation, 2002).

[4] Arizona Rural Policy Institute, *Demographic Analysis of the Navajo Nation Using 2010 Census and 2010 American Community Survey Estimates*

(Flagstaff, AZ: Center for Business Outreach W.A. Franke College of Business, Northern Arizona University, 2010).

[5] Linda Tuhiwai Smith, *Decolonizing Methodologies: Research and Indigenous Peoples* (Dunedin, New Zealand: University of Otago Press, 1999), 1.

[6] "Steve Allison," interview by author, Kayenta, AZ, July 2005.

[7] "Peter Walker," interview by author, Albuquerque, NM, August 2005.

[8] "John Brown," interview by author, Albuquerque, NM, August 8, 2007.

[9] "Phillip Lester," interview by author, Fort Wingate, NM, November 20, 2007.

[10] "Paul Yazzie," interview by author, Tempe, AZ, October 14, 2005.

[11] "Troy Mann," interview by author, Fort Wingate, NM, October 12, 2007.

[12] "Matthew Billison," interview by author, Tempe, AZ, January 13, 2006.

[13] "Frank Begay," interview by author, Phoenix, AZ, May 11, 2006.

[14] "Tom Cooper," interview by author, Tempe, AZ, January 17, 2006.

[15] "Michael Wagner," interview by author, Farmington, NM, September 28, 2007.

[16] "Gabriel Porter," interview by author, Gallup, NM, November 30, 2007.

[17] "Scott Gordon," interview by author, Albuquerque, NM, March 19, 2008.

[18] "Walter Johnson," interview by author, Lukachukai, AZ, February 11, 2006.

[19] "Steve Allison," interview by author, Kayenta, AZ, July 2005.

[20] "Peter Walker," interview by author, Albuquerque, NM, August 2005.

[21] "Hank Masters," interview by author, Albuquerque, NM, January 9, 2006.

[22] "David Francis," interview by author, Phoenix, AZ, September 14, 2005.

[23] "Brian Erickson," interview by author, Fort Wingate, NM, February 10, 2006.

[24] "Tom Cooper," interview by author, Tempe, AZ, January 17, 2006.

[25] "Frank Begay," interview by author, Phoenix, AZ, May 11, 2006.

[26] "Gary Jones," interview by author, Fort Wingate, NM, June 11, 2007.

[27] "Peter Walker," interview by author, Albuquerque, NM, August 2005.

[28] Michael Kimmel, *Manhood in America: A Cultural History* (New York: The Free Press, 1996).

[29] "Matthew Billison," interview by author, Tempe, AZ, January 13, 2006.

[30] "Peter Walker," interview by author, Albuquerque, NM, August 2005.

[31] "Steve Allison," interview by author, Kayenta, AZ, July 2005.

[32] "Matthew Billison," interview by author, Tempe, AZ, January 13, 2006.

[33] "Paul Yazzie," interview by author, Tempe, AZ, October 14, 2006.

[34] "Michael Wagner," interview by author, Farmington, NM, September 28, 2007.

[35] "Frank Begay," interview by author, Phoenix, AZ, May 11, 2006.

[36] "Peter Walker," interview by author, Albuquerque, NM, August 2005.

[37] "Steve Allison," interview by author, Kayenta, AZ, July 2005.

[38] "Frank Begay," interview by author, Phoenix, AZ, May 11, 2006.

[39] "John Brown," interview by author, Albuquerque, NM, August 8, 2007.

[40] "Phillip Lester," interview by author, Fort Wingate, NM, November 20, 2007.

[41] "Steve Allison," interview by author, Kayenta, AZ, July 2005.

[42] "Walter Johnson," interview by author, Lukachukai, AZ, February 11, 2006.

[43] "Bruce Jackson," interview by author, Fort Wingate, NM, October 8, 2007.

[44] "Troy Mann," interview by author, Fort Wingate, NM, October 12, 2007.

[45] "Steve Allison," interview by author, Kayenta, AZ, July 2005.

[46] "Brian Erickson," interview by author, Fort Wingate, NM, February 10, 2006.

[47] "Ron Palmer," interview by author, Fort Wingate, NM, October 12, 2007.

[48] "Albert Burns," interview by author, Tsaile, AZ, July 26, 2007.

[49] "Michael Wagner," interview by author, Farmington, NM, September 28, 2007.

[50] "Peter Walker," interview by author, Albuquerque, NM, August 2005.

[51] "Walter Johnson," interview by author, Lukachukai, AZ, February 11, 2006.

[52] "Frank Begay," interview by author, Phoenix, AZ, May 11, 2006.

[53] "Peter Walker," interview by author, Albuquerque, NM, August 2005.

[54] "Tom Cooper," interview by author, Tempe, AZ, January 17, 2006.

[55] "John Brown," interview by author, Albuquerque, NM, August 8, 2007.

[56] "Steve Allison," interview by author, Kayenta, AZ, July 2005.

[57] "Hank Masters," interview by author, Albuquerque, NM, January 9, 2006.

[58] "Peter Walker," interview by author, Albuquerque, NM, August 2005.

[59] "Bruce Jackson," interview by author, Fort Wingate, NM, October 8, 2007.

[60] "Gary Jones," interview by author, Fort Wingate, NM, June 11, 2007.

[61] "Steve Allison," interview by author, Kayenta, AZ, July 2005.

[62] "Steve Allison," interview by author, Kayenta, AZ, July 2005.

[63] "Gabriel Porter," interview by author, Gallup, NM, November 30, 2007.

[64] "Henry Etsitty," interview by author, Albuquerque, NM, March 26, 2008.

[65] "Gabriel Porter," interview by author, Gallup, NM, November 30, 2007.

[66] "Peter Walker," interview by author, Albuquerque, NM, August 2005.

[67] "Walter Johnson," interview by author, Lukachukai, AZ, February 11, 2006.

[68] Kimmel, "Global Masculinities: Restoration and Resistance."

Chapter 6. Hastiin: Twenty-First Century Diné Masculinities

[1] Clyde Kluckhohn, "The Philosophy of the Navaho Indians, " in *Ideological Differences and World Order*, F.S.C. Northrop, ed. (New Haven: Yale University Press, 1949), 356-383.

[2] Ibid., 377.

[3] Colleen O'Neill, *Working the Navajo Way: Labor and Culture in the Twentieth Century* (Lawrence, KS: University Press of Kansas, 2005), 108.

[4] Charlotte J. Frisbie and David P. McAllester, eds., *Navajo Blessingway Singer: The Autobiography of Frank Mitchell, 1881-1967* (Albuquerque: University of New Mexico Press, 2003), 139.

[5] Martin D. Topper, "Drinking as an Expression of Status: Navajo Male Adolescents," in *Drinking Behavior Among Southwestern Indians*, eds. Jack O. Waddell & Michael W. Everett (Tucson: University of Arizona Press, 1980), 140.

[6] Stephen J. Kunitz and Jerrold E. Levy, *Drinking, Conduct Disorder, and Social Change: Navajo Experiences* (New York: Oxford University Press, 2000), 162.

[7] Ibid., 125.

[8] Jennifer Nez Denetdale, "Chairmen, Presidents, and Princesses: The Navajo Nation, Gender, and the Politics of Tradition," *Wicazo Sa Review* 21, No. 1 (Spring 2006), 9-28.

[9] US Bureau of the Census. *The American Indian and Alaska Native Population: 2010, 2010 Census Briefs*. Prepared by the US Department of Commerce Economics and Statistics Adminstration, Bureau of the Census. Washington, DC, 2012.

[10] "Steve Allison," interview by author, Kayenta, AZ, September 8, 2006.

[11] "Brian Erickson," interview by author, Fort Wingate, NM, September 16, 2006.

[12] "Ken Lee," interview by author, Gallup, NM, January 11, 2008.

[13] "Randy Thompson," interview by author, Fort Wingate, NM, January 11, 2008.

[14] "John Brown," interview by author, Albuquerque, NM, August 20, 2007.

[15] "Frank Begay," interview by author, Phoenix, AZ, August 30, 2006.

[16] Gladys A. Reichard, *Social Life of the Navajo Indians, with some attention to minor ceremonies* (New York: Columbia University Press, 1928), 69.

[17] "Frank Begay," interview by author, Phoenix, AZ, August 30, 2006.

[18] "Bruce Jackson," interview by author, Gallup, NM, October 8, 2007.

[19] "John Brown," interview by author, Albuquerque, NM, August 20, 2007.

[20] "Brian Erickson," interview by author, Fort Wingate, NM, September 16, 2006.

[21] "Steve Allison," interview by author, Kayenta, AZ, September 8, 2006.

[22] Gary D. Sandefur and Trudy McKinnell, "American Indian Intermarriage," *Social Science Research* 15 (1986), 347-371.

[23] "Steve Allison," interview by author, Kayenta, AZ, September 8, 2006.

[24] "Frank Begay," interview by author, Phoenix, AZ, August 30, 2006.

[25] "Troy Mann," interview by author, Gallup, NM, October 12, 2007.

[26] "Michael Wagner," interview by author, Farmington, NM, September 28, 2007.

[27] "John Brown," interview by author, Albuquerque, NM, August 20, 2007.

[28] "Brian Erickson," interview by author, Fort Wingate, NM, September 16, 2006.

[29] "Randy Thompson," interview by author, Fort Wingate, NM, January 11, 2008.

[30] "Matthew Billison," interview by author, Phoenix, AZ, September 21, 2006.

[31] "Andrea Yazzie," discussion with author, Albuquerque, NM, September 11, 2006.

[32] "Vicky Charley," discussion with author, Farmington, NM, September 13, 2006.

[33] "Steve Allison," interview by author, Kayenta, AZ, September 8, 2006.

[34] "Brian Erickson," interview by author, Fort Wingate, NM, September 16, 2006.

[35] "John Brown," interview by author, Albuquerque, NM, August 20, 2007.

[36] "Andrea Yazzie," discussion with author, Albuquerque, NM, September 11, 2006.

[37] "Brian Erickson," interview by author, Fort Wingate, NM, September 16, 2006.

Chapter 7. Siihasin: Reflecting on Diné Masculinities

[1] Rex Lee Jim, "A Moment in My Life," in *Here First: Autobiographical Essays by Native American Writers*, ed. Arnold Krupat and Brian Swann (New York: The Modern Library, 2000), 233.

[2] "Peter Walker," interview by author, Albuquerque, NM, August 2005.

Selected Bibliography

Primary Source

Archives
University of New Mexico Center for Southwest Research, American Indian Oral History Collection, 1967-1972

Secondary Sources
Anderson, Kim. *Recognition of Being: Reconstructing Native Womanhood.* Toronto: Sumach Press, 2000.

Aronlith, Jr., Wilson. *Foundation of Navajo Culture.* Tsaile, AZ: Diné College, 1992.

Arthur, Claudeen, et.al. *Between Sacred Mountains: Navajo Stories and Lessons from the Land.* Tucson, AZ: University of Arizona Press, 1994.

Bahr, Howard M. *Diné Bibliography to the 1990s: A Companion to the Navajo Bibliography of 1969.* Lanham, MD: Scarecrow Press, 1999.

Bailey, Garrick, and Roberta Glenn Bailey. *A History of the Navajos: The Reservation Years.* Santa Fe, NM: School of American Research, 1986.

Bailey, Lynn Robinson. *Indian Slave Trade in the Southwest: A Study of Slave-Taking and the Traffic in Indian Captives.* Los Angeles, CA: Westernlore Press, 1966.

Begay, Shirley M. *Kinaalda: A Navajo Puberty Ceremony.* Rough Rock, AZ: Navajo Curriculum Center, Rough Rock Demonstration School, 1983.

Benally, Herbert J. "Navajo Philosophy of Learning and Pedagogy." *Journal of Navajo Education* XIII, no.1 (Fall 1994): 23-31.

Bighorse, Tiana. *Bighorse the Warrior.* Edited by Noel Bennett. Tucson, AZ: University of Arizona Press, 1990.

Bitsilly, Dorothy. "Navajo Leadership." *Leading the Way: The Wisdom of the Navajo People* 6, no. 12 (December 2008): 15,18-20.

Bonvillain, Nancy. "Gender Relations in Native North America." *American Indian Culture and Research Journal* 13, no. 2 (1989): 1-28.

Brooks, James F. *Captives and Cousins: Slavery, Kinship and Community in the Southwest Borderlands*. Chapel Hill, NC: University of Carolina Press, 2002.

Brugge, David M. "Navajo Archaeology: A Promising Past." In Ronald H. Towner, ed., *The Archaeology of Navajo Origins*. Salt Lake City, UT: University of Utah Press, 1996.

----------------. *Navajos in the Catholic Church Records of New Mexico, 1694-1875*. Tsaile, AZ: Navajo Community College Press, 1985.

----------------. "Navajo Prehistory and History to 1850." In Alfonso Ortiz and William C. Sturtevant, eds., *Handbook of North American Indians Volume 10: Southwest*. Washington, DC: Smithsonian Institution, 1983.

Burn, Shawn Meghan and A. Zachary Ward. "Men's Conformity to Traditional Masculinity and Relationship Satisfaction." *Psychology of Men and Masculinity* 6, no. 4 (2005): 254-263.

Burstyn, Varda. *The Rites of Men: Manhood, Politics, and the Culture of Sport*. Toronto: University of Toronto Press, 1999.

Caffrey, Margaret M. "Complementary Power: Men and Women of the Lenni Lenape." *American Indian Quarterly* 24, no. 1 (Winter 2000): 44-63.

Chamberlain, Kathleen P. *Under Sacred Ground: A History of Navajo Oil 1922-1982*. Albuquerque, NM: University of New Mexico Press, 2000.

Choudhary, Trib. *Navajo Nation Data from US Census 2000*. Window Rock, AZ: Division of Economic Development, 2002.

Clark, LaVerne Harrell. *They Sang For Horses: The Impact of the Horse on Navajo and Apache Folklore*. Boulder, CO: University Press of Colorado, 2001.

Clinton, Verna. *Ashkii's Journey*. Flagstaff, AZ: Salina Bookshelf, Inc., 2001.

Connell, R.W. *Masculinities*. Berkeley, CA: University of California Press, 1995.

Denetdale, Jennifer Nez. "Chairmen, Presidents, and Princesses: The Navajo Nation, Gender, and the Politics of Tradition." *Wicazo Sa Review* 21, no. 1 (Spring 2006): 9-28.

----------------. *Reclaiming Diné History: The Legacies of Navajo Chief Manuelito and Juanita*. Tucson, AZ: University of Arizona Press, 2007.

---------------. "Representing Changing Woman: A Review Essay on Navajo Women." *American Indian Culture and Research Journal* 25, no. 3 (2001): 1-26.

Dyk, Walter. *Son of Old Man Hat: A Navaho Autobiography*. Lincoln, NE: University of Nebraska Press, 1967.

Edwards, Tim. *Cultures of Masculinity*. London: Routledge, 2006.

Farella, John R. *The Main Stalk: A Synthesis in Navajo Philosophy*. Albuquerque, NM: University of New Mexico Press, 1984.

Faris, James C. *Navajo and Photography: A Critical History of the Representation of an American People*. Albuquerque, NM: University of New Mexico Press, 1996.

Franciscan Fathers. *An Ethnological Dictionary of the Navaho Language*. St. Michaels, AZ: St. Michaels Press, 1910.

Frisbie, Charlotte. *Kinaalda: A Study of the Navaho Girl's Puberty Ceremony*. Salt Lake City, UT: University of Utah Press, 1993.

Fuller, Norma. "The Social Constitution of Gender Identity among Peruvian Men." *Men and Masculinities* 3, no. 3 (January 2001): 316-331.

Gavanas, Anne. *Fatherhood Politics in the United States: Masculinity, Sexuality, Race, and Marriage*. Urbana, IL: University of Illinois Press, 2004.

Goffman, Erving. *Stigma: Notes on the Management of Spoiled Identity*. Englewood Cliffs, NJ: Prentice Hall, 1963.

Griffin-Pierce, Trudy. *Earth is my Mother, Sky if my Father: Space, Time, and Astronomy in Navajo Sandpainting*. Albuquerque, NM: University of New Mexico Press, 1992.

Grinde, Donald A. and Bruce E. Johansen. *Ecocide of Native America: Environmental Destruction of Indian Lands and Peoples*. Santa Fe, NM: Clear Light Publishers, 1995.

Haile, Father Berard. *Origin Legends of the Navajo Enemyway*. New Haven, CT: Yale University Press, 1938.

Haile, Father Berard, recorder. *Women versus Men: A Conflict of Navajo Emergence/The Curly to Aheedliinii Version*. Edited by Karl W. Luckert. Lincoln, NE: University of Nebraska Press, 1981.

Haskie, Miranda J. "Preserving a Culture: Practicing the Navajo Principles of Hózhǫ́ dóó K'é." Ph.D. diss., Fielding Graduate Institute, 2002.

Henderson, Eric, Stephen J. Kunitz and Jerrold E. Levy. "The Origins of Navajo Youth Gangs." *American Indian Culture and Research Journal* 23, no. 3 (1999): 243-264.

Hoffman, Virginia and Broderick H. Johnson. *Navajo Biographies*. Rough Rock, AZ: Navajo Curriculum Center, 1970.

Hokowhitu, Brendon. "Tackling Maori Masculinity: A Colonial Genealogy of Savagery and Sport." *The Contemporary Pacific* 16, no. 2 (Fall 2004):259-284.

----------------. "Maori Masculinity, Post-structuralism, and the Emerging Self." *New Zealand Sociology* 18, no. 2 (2003): 179-201.

Holiday, John and Robert S. McPherson. *A Navajo Legacy: The Life and Teachings of John Holiday*. Norman, OK: University of Oklahoma Press, 2005.

hooks, bell. *The Will to Change: Men, Masculinity, and Love*. New York, NY: Atria Books, 2004.

Iverson, Peter. *Diné: A History of the Navajos*. Albuquerque, NM: University of New Mexico Press, 2002.

----------------, ed. *"For our Navajo People": Diné Letters, Speeches, and Petitions 1900-1960*. Albuquerque, NM: University of New Mexico Press, 2002.

Jett, Stephen C. "Pete Price, Navajo Medicineman (1868-1951): A Brief Biography." *American Indian Quarterly* Winter 1991: 91-103.

Jim, Rex Lee. "A Moment in My Life." In Arnold Krupat and Brian Swann, eds., *Here First: Autobiographical Essays by Native American Writers*. New York, NY: The Modern Library, 2000.

Johnson, Broderick H. *Navajos and World War II*. Tsaile, AZ: Navajo Community College Press, 1977.

----------------. *Navajo Stories of the Long Walk Period*. Tsaile, AZ: Navajo Community College Press, 1973.

----------------. *Stories of Traditional Navajo Life and Culture*. Tsaile, AZ: Navajo Community College Press, 1977.

Kammer, Jerry. "New, Unifying Ritual: 'Rezball'." *Arizona Republic*, September 1993.

Kehily, Mary. "Bodies in School: Young Men, Embodiment, and Heterosexual Masculinities." *Men and Masculinities* 4, no. 2 (October 2001): 173-185.

Keith, Anne. "The Navajo Girl's Puberty Ceremony: Function and Meaning for the Adolescent." *El Palacio* 71, no. 1: 27-36.

Kelly, Klara and Harris Francis. "Anthropological Traditions versus Navajo Traditions about early Navajo history." In Meliha S. Duran and David T. Kirkpatrick, eds., *Diné Bikéyah: Papers in Honor of David M. Brugge*. Series No. 24, Albuquerque, NM: Archaeological Society of New Mexico, 1998.

Kimmel, Michael S., Jeff Hearn, and R. W. Connell. *Handbook of Studies on Men and Masculinities*. Thousands Oaks, CA: SAGE Publications, Inc., 2005.

Kimmel, Michael. "Global Masculinities: Restoration and Resistance." *Gender Policy Review* (November 2000).

----------------. *Manhood in America: A Cultural History*. New York, NY: The Free Press, 1996.

Kluckhohn, Clyde. "The Philosophy of the Navaho Indians." In F.S.C. Northrop, ed., *Ideological Differences and World Order*. New Haven, CT: Yale University Press, 1949.

Kunitz, Stephen J. and Jerrold E. Levy. *Drinking, Conduct Disorder, and Social Change: Navajo Experience*. Oxford: Oxford University Press, 2000.

Lee, Anthony. "My Male Puberty Ceremony: Yilzííh." *Leading the Way: The Wisdom of the Navajo People* 7, no. 8 (August 2009): 2-5.

Leighton, Alexander. *Lucky the Navajo Singer*. Edited by Joyce J. Griffen. Albuquerque, NM: University of New Mexico Press, 1992.

Leighton, Dorothea and Clyde Kluckhohn. *Children of the People: The Navaho Individual and His Development*. Cambridge, MA: Harvard University Press, 1947.

Levy, Jerrold E. *In the Beginning: The Navajo Genesis*. Berkeley, CA: University of California Press, 1998.

Locke, Raymond Friday. *The Book of the Navajo*. Los Angeles, CA: Mankind Press, 1992.

Lopez, Antoinette Sedillo. "Evolving Indigenous Law: Navajo Marriage-Cultural Traditions and Modern Challenges." *Arizona Journal of International and Comparative Law* 17, no. 2 (2000): 283-308.

Matlock, Marci. "Sa'ah Naaghai Bik'eh Hozhoon: Tapping into the Power of Words." *Journal of Navajo Education* 12, no. 3 (Spring 1995): 19-24.

Matthews, Washington, collector and trans. *Navaho Legends*. 1897. Reprint, Salt Lake City, UT: University of Utah Press, 2002.

McEachern, Diane, Marlene Van Winkle, and Sue Steiner. "Domestic Violence among the Navajo: A Legacy of Colonization." *Journal of Poverty* 2, no. 4 (September 1998): 31-46.

McNeley, James Kale. *Holy Wind in Navajo Philosophy*. Tucson, AZ: University of Arizona Press, 1981.

McNitt, Frank. *Navajo Wars: Military Campaigns, Slave Raids, and Reprisals*. Albuquerque, NM: University of New Mexico Press, 1990.

McPherson, Robert S. *The Journey of Navajo Oshley: An Autobiography and Life History*. Logan, UT: Utah State University Press, 2000.

---------------. *Navajo Land, Navajo Culture: The Utah Experience in the Twentieth Century*. Norman, OK: University of Oklahoma Press, 2001.

Messner, Michael. "Boyhood, Organized Sports, and the Construction of Masculinities." *Journal of Contemporary Ethnography* 18, no. 4 (1990): 416-444.

Messner, Michael and Donald F. Sabo. *Sex, Violence, and Power in Sports: Rethinking Masculinity*. Berkeley, CA: Crossing Press, 1994.

Mirande, Alfredo. *Hombres y Machos: Masculinity and Latino Culture*. Boulder, CO: Westview Press, 1997.

Mitchell, Blackhorse. *Miracle Hill: The Story of a Navajo Boy*. Tucson, AZ: University of Arizona Press, 2004.

Mitchell, Frank. *Navajo Blessingway Singer: The Autobiography of Frank Mitchell, 1881-1967*. Edited by Charlotte J. Frisbie and David P. McAllester. Albuquerque, NM: University of New Mexico Press, 2003.

Mitchell, Rose. *Tall Woman: The Life Story of Rose Mitchell, A Navajo Woman, c. 1874-1977*. Edited by Charlotte J. Frisbie. Albuquerque, NM: University of New Mexico Press, 2001.

Morris, Irvin. *From the Glittering World: A Navajo Story*. Norman, OK: University of Oklahoma Press, 1997.

Newcomb, Franc Johnson. *Hosteen Klah: Navaho Medicine Man and Sand Painter*. Norman, OK: University of Oklahoma Press, 1964.

New Mexico Department of Cultural Affairs. *The Story of Bosque Redondo*. 2005.

O'Bryan, Aileen. *Navaho Indian Myths*. 1956. Reprint, New York, NY: Dover, 1993.

O'Neill, Colleen. *Working the Navajo Way: Labor and Culture in the Twentieth Century*. Lawrence, KS: University Press of Kansas, 2005.

Parr, Joy. "Gender History and Historical Practice." *Canadian Historical Review* 76, no. 3 (1995): 354-376.

Ramirez, Rafael L. and Rosa E. Capser. *What It Means to be a Man: Reflections on Puerto Rican Masculinity*. New Brunswick, NJ: Rutgers University Press, 1999.

Reichard, Gladys A. *Social Life of the Navajo Indians, with some attention to minor ceremonies*. New York, NY: AMS Press, 1969.

---------------. *Navaho Religion: A Study of Symbolism*. New York, NY: Pantheon, 1950.

Roessel, Robert A., Jr. *Navajo Education, 1948-1978: Its Progress and Its Problems*. Rough Rock, AZ: Navajo Curriculum Center, 1979.

Roessel, Ruth. *Women in Navajo Society*. Rough Rock, AZ: Navajo Resource Center, 1981.

Said, Edward S. *Orientalism*. New York, NY: Vintage Books, 1979.

Salaybe, Jr., John E. and Kathleen Manolescu. "The Beginnings of Marriage and Family: Corn Story Teachings." *Leading the Way: The Wisdom of the Navajo People* 6, no. 11 (November 2008): 2-5.

Sandefur, Gary D. and Trudy McKinnell. "American Indian Intermarriage." *Social Science Research* 15 (1986): 347-371.

Sanghani, Zarana. "Descendants of the Anasazi?" *Gallup Independent*, April 2000.

Schwarz, Maureen Trudelle. *Molded in the Image of Changing Woman: Navajo Views on the Human Body and Personhood*. Tucson, AZ: University of Arizona Press, 1997.

Smith, Linda Tuhiwai. *Decolonizing Methodologies: Research and Indigenous Peoples*. New York, NY: St. Martin's Press, 1999.

Spicer, Edward H. *Cycles of Conquest: The Impact of Spain, Mexico, and the United States on the Indians of the Southwest, 1533-1960*. Tucson, AZ: University of Arizona Press, 1962.

Steinberg, Warren. *Masculinity: Identity Conflict and Transformation*. Boston, MA: Shambhala, 1993.

Tapahonoso, Luci. *Saanii Dahataal: The Women are Singing*. Tucson, AZ: University of Arizona Press, 1993.

Tengan, Ty P. Kawika. "Hale Mua: (En)Gendering Hawaiian Men." Ph.D. diss., University of Hawai'i, 2003.

---------------. *Native Men Remade: Gender and Nation in Contemporary Hawai'i*. Durham, NC: Duke University Press, 2008.

Thom, Laine. *Becoming Brave: The Path to Native American Manhood*. San Francisco, CA: Chronicle Books, 1992.

Thomas, Wesley. "Navajo Cultural Constructions." In *Two-Spirit People: Native American Gender Identity, Sexuality, and Spirituality*. Urbana: University of Illinois Press, 1997.

Thompson, Hildegard. *The Navajos' Long Walk for Education: A History of Navajo Education*. Tsaile, AZ: Navajo Community Press, 1975.

Topper, Martin D. "Drinking as an Expression of Status: Navajo Male Adolescents." In Jack O. Waddell and Michael W. Everett, eds., *Drinking Behavior Among Southwestern Indians*. Tucson, AZ: University of Arizona Press, 1980.

Topper, Martin D. and G. Mark Schoepfle. "Becoming a Medicine Man: A Means to Successful Midlife Transition among Traditional Navajo Men." In Calvin A. Colarusso and Robert A. Nemiroff, eds., *New Dimensions in Adult Development*. New York, NY: Basic Books, 1990.

Tsinnajinnie, Leola Roberta. "Examining the Indigenous Relationship Between Education and the United States' Military from 2001-2009." Ph.D. diss., University of New Mexico, 2011.

Underhill, Ruth M. *The Navajos*. Norman, OK: University of Oklahoma Press, 1956.

Vigoya, Mara Viveros. "Contemporary Latin American Perspectives on Masculinity." *Men and Masculinities* 3, no. 3 (January 2001): 237-260.

Wakefield, Wanda Ellen. *Playing to Win: Sports and the American Military, 1898-1945*. Albany, NY: State University of New York Press, 1997.

Witherspoon, Gary. *Language and Art in the Navajo Universe*. Ann Arbor, MI: The University of Michigan Press, 1977.

---------------. *Navajo Kinship and Marriage*. Chicago, IL: University of Chicago Press, 1975.

Wilkins, David E. *The Navajo Political Experience*. Lanham, MD: Rowman and Littlefield Publishers, Inc., 2003.

Woodsum, Jo Ann. "Gender & Sexuality in Native American Societies: A Bibliography." *American Indian Quarterly* 19, no. 4 (Fall 1995): 527-554.

Wyman, Leland and Flora Bailey. "Navaho Girl's Puberty Rite." *New Mexico Anthropologist* 15, no. 1: 3-12.

Yazzie, Ethelou, ed. *Navajo History Volume I.* Chinle, AZ: Rough Rock Press, 1971.

Zion, James W. and Elsie B. Zion. "Hozho' Sokee'—Stay Together Nicely: Domestic Violence Under Navajo Common Law." *Arizona State Law Journal* 25 (1993): 407-426.

Zolbrod, Paul. *Diné Bahane': The Navajo Creation Story.* Albuquerque, NM: University of New Mexico Press, 1984.

Index

About the Author

L loyd L. Lee is a citizen of the Navajo Nation and of the Kinyaa'áanii (Towering House) clan, born for the Tł'ááschíí (Red Bottom) clan. His maternal grandfather clan is Áshįįhí (Salt) and his paternal grandfather clan is Tábąąhá (Water's Edge).

Originally from Albuquerque, NM, he went to Dartmouth College and graduated in 1994 with B.A. in History. He then went onto Stanford University where he received his M.A. in Education in 1995. From 1995 to 1999, he taught Social Studies at Wingate High School (a Bureau of Indian Affairs boarding school) at Fort Wingate, NM. After teaching for four years, he returned to school at the University of New Mexico, and earned his Ph.D. in American Studies in 2004.

His research areas include indigenous and Diné identity, indigenous and Diné masculinities, Diné transformative research, indigenous leadership development, indigenous matrices, and indigenous community building. He has published articles in *The American Indian Quarterly*, *Wicazo Sa Review*, *AlterNative: An International Journal of Indigenous Peoples*, *The International Journal of the Sociology of Language*, and *Indigenous Policy Journal*.